St. Louis Community College

Forest Park
Florissant Valley
Meramec

Instructional Resources
St. Louis, Missouri

GAYLORD

MALE CODE

MALE CODE

RULES MEN LIVE AND LOVE BY

TWYMAN L. TOWERY

Glenbridge Publishing Ltd.

Library of Congress Catalog Card Number: LC 91-77118

International Standard Book Number: 0-944435-17-3

CONTENTS

To my parents

FOREWORD

Around the turn of the 20th century, Sigmund Freud advanced theories destined to impact on the entire world. His psychological hypotheses were embraced eagerly as the key to why we behave and react as we do as adults. Freud's theories now permeate all areas of life having given birth to "the code" that Dr. Towery so ably explores. Freudian terminology has become part of our everyday language—ego, super ego, the id, father figure, mother figure, and oedipal complex. His ideas are used even today to defend our welfare programs and public and mental health approaches. Though many of Freud's hypotheses have been superseded by other discoveries, his concepts of how we are reared as children have a significant impact on how we behave and interact as adults.

The code imposed upon men often leads to an inability to express true feelings in compelling situations such as a love/marriage relationship. How can they show their feelings openly in business situations where they always are expected to be strong and a winner?

Lucky is the man who can break through the code and be himself, to be comfortable with himself without the need for evasion, pretense, or deception. The man who has at least partially broken the code may be able to take emotional onslaught in stride.

As Dr. Towery points out, the male code is probably stronger and more restrictive than the female code, though women struggle with their code as well. Their codes are less confining, however, as they relate to the true expression of emotion.

While we cannot change our genetic code, we can change our psychological code. It is also safe to say that we never totally eliminate the way we feel as a result of our environmental upbringing.

We can gain valuable insight, however, and that is what Dr. Towery's book provides so well. As much as any book I have ever read, *Male Code* will go a long way toward making us more comfortable in dealing with interpersonal and human relationships.

Nat T. Winston, M.D.,
Chairman, CareNet, Inc., Nashville, Tennessee,
Former Commissioner of Mental Health for the State of Tennessee

PREFACE

"So what do I have to do to have male friends again," I mused with my friend, an outstanding New Orleans psychotherapist. "Advertise for them?"

We both had a big laugh. And then suddenly it wasn't that funny. To be in your forties and discover that you have few, if any, real male friends is quite a shock to most men.

But that's exactly what happens. Sure, we have hunting acquaintances, business acquaintances, and exercising and drinking and football-watching acquaintances, but often not a single one feels like a friend in the sense of the word that we knew as a kid.

I found that the same person who would perfunctorily write down the time and date for our next match in his appointment book would have a medium-sized stress attack if I called him up out of the blue to suggest we have lunch. "Why?" "What for?" "What do you want to talk about?" I could almost hear these thoughts through the silence on the phone. And yet — women call each other regularly. For no purpose at all. No goal or objective. Just friendship. Well, how silly. What a waste of time!

Boy, did I envy them!

So after our nervous laughter was over, we compared notes on what we knew about the state of the modern American male and decided that, all in all, it was a pretty dreary picture. Many women like to talk about how it's a man's world, but after looking at the facts, you have to conclude it's a world few men would choose. Whether it's heart disease, suicide, alcoholism, drug abuse, or any other bad category you can think of, men generally lead the pack.

That conversation was a turning point in my life. As crazy as it sounded at first, I decided that I would advertise for male friends. I would just have to find a unique way to do it, and maybe help today's American males at the same time.

The answer I came up with became the newspaper column, *MaleCall,* a question-and-answer column that allows both men and women to share their questions, feelings, opinions, fears, and suggestions on a subject that affects us all to one degree or another — MEN.

For a long time I've noticed, especially when attending various psychology seminars and workshops, that conversations between men and women, and women and women, always seem to gravitate toward women. Conversations between men and men (when they happen) tend to be about objects or activities instead of themselves. You rarely hear conversations about men, particularly from women, unless it's time to dish out some criticism. "Men are insensitive." "Men can't communicate." "All men want is a mother to pick up after them." "I don't blame men for wanting a wife. I'd want one too if she would do all the stuff I have to do." And while I don't deny that women have a tremendously heavy burden to bear, so do men.

But I've observed that if a man verbalized some of his frustrations with life, he was often greeted with rolled eyes and yawns until the conversation turned to some feminine topic.

In my own case, I was beginning to feel a little like the title of the Lewis Grizzard book, *Elvis Is Dead and I Don't Feel So Good Myself.* I began researching the literature relating to men, but quickly realized you can't research men without concurrently studying women. This is helpful in some ways, as one can sometimes get a clear picture about how the sexes operate with each other. But I also wanted to know how men themselves operate. What makes us tick?

Several feminist friends helped me out by pointing me in the direction of research on the sexes. Books, articles, and tapes from hundreds of interviews began lining my library shelves. I was increasingly struck by the profound differences between men and women. You name it — psychologically, emotionally, mentally — we're very different creatures.

One of the most fundamental differences, I discovered, is the unspoken "Code" men live by. The Code is passed down from one generation to the next; it consists of a long list of outdated messages that keep men immobilized emotionally. It affects every aspect of our lives, and certainly the people who work with us and have relationships with us (i.e., women, kids).

Some components of The Code are positive: "Always be a man of your word," and other worthy behavior. But the majority of the rules prescribes strong, silent, and confident behavior at all costs. In a word, too many men think they're supposed to go it alone, like Dirty Harry.

And we die approximately 7.5 years earlier for it.

It took my emotionally frustrated outburst with my psychotherapist friend to show me how to use this information for my own benefit and, if the response from my newspaper column, radio, and TV shows is any guide, there are legions of others who feel the same way. It hasn't always been easy. Newspapers were originally afraid that women wouldn't read about men, or that men wouldn't read about men, or that feminist groups would resent the showing of any sympathy toward men. They were wrong.

From the first I was struck with how helpful and supportive women were of the concept. Many went out of their way to let me know how important they thought it was that men's issues were being discussed, just as women's have been. The health editor of *The Trenton Times,* Robin Lichtenstein, summed it up nicely when her paper decided to begin running my column, saying, "Every cell and molecule of today's female has been dissected and analyzed, while all we hear about men is how often they can or can't get it up. Our readers want a glimpse into the hearts of men."

And so, I found, does everyone. Let's take a look.

I would like to thank Bonnie Arnett for her valuable assistance in writing this book.

INTRODUCTION

THE SPELL OF THE MALE CODE

"A man in armor is his armor's slave."
                                    — Robert Browning

American men today live under the rule of The Male Code. The Code is extremely powerful, yet few recognize its force or vigilance.

We've heard about "the new man." He's the perfect guy — sensitive and caring — yet strong. He has the courage to recognize his feelings and articulate them without coming across as a softie. He isn't pushy or selfish. I'm as big a fan of his as anyone. I love watching "the new man" on TV and in the movies. And some of us even think we've shed our Cro-Magnon persona. But let's ask ourselves just how far men really have progressed.

Many of us believe that M*A*S*H hero Hawkeye Pierce is the personification of the new man. If you ask women what they like about Hawkeye, you are going to hear words like: sensitive, cute, vulnerable, witty.

On closer scrutiny, however, Hawkeye embodies The Code. He is commitment-phobic. Oh, he has sex. He constantly talks to women, though banter is a better word for it. But it is always on his terms, his timetable — never leaving any doubt that he is not going to commit to anything. With one exception. He is committed to being a great physician. He is committed to his work. Hawkeye doesn't really need women; he uses them. He doesn't really need anyone — just his martinis. He certainly doesn't need the army. He hates it and pushes against the grain every chance he gets.

Most men still sit as observers in their own family circle. From the time they're mothered until the time they're married, they allow the female to assume the expressive role. Women end up interpreting for the rest of the family. "What your father really means is . . ." "Well, you know your Daddy loves you, he just has a hard time saying so. . . ."

Men, as a rule, participate in the family to the extent that they fulfill tasks. They think of their primary role as breadwinner, problem-solver, the strong silent tower of answers. "Dad isn't supposed to be depressed," is the message we hear. "Dad isn't supposed to cry. And Dad sure isn't supposed to ever shake his head and say, "I don't know."

There is certainly a part of us that makes us like, even relish this image from time to time. So what's the matter?

Take a moment and see if the following questions also strike a familiar chord:

- Do you ever wake up in the middle of the night, thinking that all will be lost if you fail at your job?
- Do you often feel as if you are walking through life with a mask on, pretending to conform and to live up to a masculine ideal?
- Do you remember learning early on that real men stand alone and like it?
- Is it difficult for you to show genuine affection to your female partner or children?
- Do you stop short of saying, "I love you," preferring instead to express love through actions?
- Can you really be comfortable with a woman's success?
- Do you view yourself as the primary wage earner?
- Is it difficult, if not impossible, for you to believe that your female partner will continue to love and/or respect you if you become impotent?
- Do you equate lovability with performance?
- Do you have difficulty trusting others, including your wife and "best" male friends?

- Do you think it is always best to err on the side of silence, and find yourself holding back sensitive information that might help others to understand you?
- Are you ashamed of others seeing you when you are obviously hurting inside, so you make a point of masking your feelings or just being alone?
- Deep inside, are you afraid of letting others share your dreams because they might laugh at you? Because they might think you're less of a man?
- Do you think your female partner thinks you place more emphasis on her aging than you in fact do?

Many men today exude a confident, upbeat, secure persona. Isn't that what everyone wants? Absolutely. Until people realize the price they are paying. The price of living by The Code is high for it means women are living with men they don't understand. Children are growing up without ever really knowing their fathers. And men are so busy trying to fool everyone that they invariably end up fooling themselves.

The Code doesn't necessarily make you more of a man; it can make you less of one. As Robert Browning noted a century ago, "a man in armor is his armor's slave." A man who models his behavior under the dictates of The Code may one day discover that being male is very self-limiting.

Stop for a minute and consider the last emotionally-charged incident in your life. Let's say you were fired two weeks ago. If you're a man who lives under The Code, you ask yourself: "What should a man do under these circumstances?" The answer is simple: Take it on the chin. Don't flinch. Let no one know how badly it hurts.

But think of what this man is denying in himself — the fear, the pain, the isolation.

For the female reader, the questions to be considered are quite different:

- Do you find yourself wishing that the man in your life was more sensitive and loving?
- Do you find yourself feeling superior to him in terms of your giving, caring nature?
- Do you find yourself thinking it's dangerous for the woman to be the primary wage earner?
- Do you have difficulty finding a way to his vulnerable or feeling side?
- Are you left thinking that your male partner doesn't share his intimate feelings with you?
- Are you tired of your husband giving all of his best energy to his work and then coming home and treating you and the children like *you* are the invaders?
- Are you tired of your male partner acting macho to the point that he won't go to the doctor even if his guts are spilling out?
- Are you aware that your partner is probably more sensitive to his own signs of aging than yours?
- Are you tired of taking care of all the details of your social life?
- Do you often catch yourself acting as interpreter between your children and their father?
- In the work place, are you convinced men conspire to hold women back?
- Do you think men in the work place are always willing to help another man (their buddies) — but not a woman?
- Are you seeing more men who view achievement-oriented women as trophies?
- In general, do you think men are far less sensitive creatures who expect women to pick up all the pieces?

If you answered "yes" to five or more of the above questions, this book is written for you. It is designed as a guide to understanding men — men governed by The Code.

And if you fit the profile of a woman who wants change, it's important that you really mean it. The media, even society at large, is hitting men with hefty double messages. Society today seems to urge a man to bare his emotions and then calls him a "wimp" when he does. The contradiction between what many women say they want and what they often choose, leaves men in a state of frustrated retreat.

For the women who truly want to see a change for the better, this book will help you to decipher the secret language of The Code. A number of male expressions is included that will help you to understand what a man really means when he says: "I hate my job." "You don't understand me." "I don't think you're handling the children well." It will not only tell you how to understand a man's language better, but also tell you what steps promote change.

In the end, the most important question the female reader can ask herself is: If I love my husband, my boyfriend, why am I reinforcing The Code? Or, if I love my son(s), why am I reinforcing these messages?

Through firsthand accounts this book will illustrate what actions — and what language — nurture the same old negative patterns in men. It also specifically identifies what you can do to let go of the male myths that ensnare all of us.

How can you know for certain if a man is caught up in The Code? The following checklist provides insight:

- Do you find yourself looking at the man you love, or live with, and saying, "I don't really know him"?
- Similarly, do you find yourself thinking, "And he can't really know me, either — he's never taken the time. He never asks me how I really feel about anything"?
- Do you often see your male partner exhibiting one side of himself to certain male friends, and a very different side to other male friends?
- Does your career present a catch-22 in your relationship? Do you feel that your partner wants you to achieve success, but not to the point where his male ego is threatened?

- If you are married, do you find your husband feels he's fulfilled his side of the obligations if he brings home a decent paycheck and is simply "there" in the home?
- If you have children, do you find yourself wishing your husband would interact more with you and the kids? That he'd be more expressive?
- If you have sons, do you see them exhibiting the old macho behavior, such as a fascination for war games, even though you have tried to rear them as a sensitive "new man"? More importantly, are you secretly glad?
- Do you wish your husband would share his most intimate secrets and dreams with you, only to find him clam up when you introduce the subject?
- If your male partner has a spell of impotence, does he act as if all is lost, that his very manhood is in jeopardy?
- Do you hold out dual messages to men, saying in one breath that you appreciate sensitivity, but rewarding men (even little boys) when they are self-charging macho types?

Most women answer "yes" to several of these questions, and that means they are confronting The Code. Beneath the confident, fun-loving exterior of the "new man" lives the real one, the haunted man. And I think that on an intuitive level, most women know this.

Generations of role expectations and myths have created men who are compelled to keep feelings inside — at all costs. They may be surrounded by the trappings of success, but on the inside, it's Skid Row. The take-charge, "I can handle it" persona becomes an unfunny, even fatal joke.

Friendship, particularly male friendship, eludes most men today. The impact of this is staggering. It ends up affecting the women, children, and parents in their lives.

This book is not about how blame can be leveled at women or men. There have been enough books blaming one or the other of the sexes (mostly men) for all of society's ills. These efforts are stupendously transparent and counterproductive. Rather, this book is about increasing understanding and empathy between the two sexes, and increasing empathy and understanding among men themselves.

This book is about how these two very different sexes can succeed together — fathers and daughters, mothers and sons, husbands and wives, female and male work partners. It's about escaping the lie of The Code.

CHAPTER ONE

THE DISAPPEARING ACT

Question for women: Are you tired of your husband giving all of his best energy to his work and then coming home and treating you and the children like you are the invaders?

For many women there is a growing frustration on the home front. Married with children, they discover that they can't reach out to the man they once knew. The question I hear over and over again is: How can I reach him?

The underlying problem hinges on one of the strongest dictates of The Code, which is "Silence is a primary virtue." This means the man is going to pretend everything is okay. In his mind, nothing is wimpier than complaining, than whining about dissatisfaction. After all, real men don't have problems they can't solve. In fact, if confronted with the issue, they will usually respond with anger.

The following letter is a case in point:

Dear Dr. Towery:

I married a math genius. In graduate school, "Larry" was wonderful — everything I dreamed of in a partner. He was confident, positive, full of dreams he was sure he knew how to attain.

Now I live with a stranger. Larry's almost forty. He's stuck in an accounting job he hates. He's given up on his dream of owning his own company. He comes home later and later. My "genius" watches countless hours of TV, and his only ambition at home is to zone out.

9

What is more confusing is that his secretary tells me he's the biggest practical joker in the office. She admires his wit! I haven't seen him laugh, really laugh, in years. Why do I never see this side of him anymore?

If I confront him about it, he mumbles something about "security and a special niche" he's developed at the Big Five firm he works for. Or worse, he lashes out at me and says I expect too much — that he does the best he can for me and the kids.

The idea of seeing a counselor makes him shudder and huff out of the room. But I want the old Larry back. Where did he go? I have several women friends in much the same boat. Can you help?

Where did he go?

I have received hundreds of letters from female readers almost identical to the one above, asking for help with this same problem. The letters are touching but filled with a growing frustration. Each of these women want to know what happened to the man they fell in love with. They wonder if he is still possibly rummaging around somewhere inside. And most importantly, they want to know how to get him back.

There is some good news and bad news. The good news: Larry's still in there. The bad news? Getting him back out is another matter entirely, and you've got a lot to work against. The solution has to begin with an understanding of how and why the old Larry came to be buried in the first place.

The Larrys of the world are caught up in The Code. And they see no way out.

These are the same clean-shaven men who drive to work each morning in their polished cars — all pistons firing — looking for all the world as if they love the system. If they smell the roses along the way, they never say so. If they flinch at the thought of another savage day at the office, they don't let on. Better to grow an ulcer than to confess feeling burned out.

But a man can wake up one morning and find that he is beginning to feel haunted by these very feelings he's denied. The mask is still in place, and the rule of the day — silence — is still Prime Operative #1. But inside, there are some scary things going on. Many women sense this as a smoldering anger.

These are the same men, you must keep in mind, that women are repeatedly telling me they don't understand and don't know. In workshops and during interviews, I hear a common refrain: "I can't talk to him. He won't communicate. He doesn't share his feelings with me." Women are frustrated and rightly so.

To the world, these men put on a brave face. On the surface, they appear calm, tackling the male gender's problem-solving duties with an old school *noblesse oblige*. But inside, where no one's allowed, they repeat a roster of inadequacies to themselves. And they pray that they're never found out — as the following letter indicates:

Dear Dr. Towery:

I'm reluctant to write. But in a way, it's safer to write than to talk face to face.

I work all the time. I make a lot of money and my family lives well. But, I feel like they aren't "my family." It's like I plug in "the image of being a dad" before I walk through the door and it's one endless game of faking it.

I love them. I really do. I just have a nagging feeling that they don't know me. Don't want to know me. I mean, what would my little girl do if I told her I thought I was going to lose my shit and get fired and then she couldn't swim at the club anymore? Or, what would my wife do if I said, "you tote the load, I can't take it anymore"? I think she would leave me for another man who could handle it.

Does everyone feel their family is so tenuous — that they can't really connect? Other men I work with always act like everything is going their way and that it always will. Am I an insecure freak?

Brad

No, Brad isn't a freak. A great number of men feel apart from the very family they love. They consider themselves interlopers in the world of feelings. They don't feel they quite belong.

But it isn't necessary to feel this way. Brad needs to take a hard look at his reactions with his family. If he thinks he is fooling his daughter into believing that everything is okay, he's wrong. Children can smell insincerity a mile away. Furthermore, children prefer to know what is going on. And while you have to protect them in certain instances, this doesn't mean treating them like emotional idiots.

The same is undoubtedly true for his wife. She probably senses his anxiety — and anger — at some level. Certain things need to be discussed in a family, and one is what would happen in the event of illness or death. If this man has never broached this discussion, then he is wrongfully presuming that his wife is only there so long as he is a decent breadwinner. Whether that is true or not, he needs to know.

Most men believe they will only be loved so long as they are performing well, whether it be in making money, having sex or being an interesting conversationalist. A useless man has no value, no reason for being. They take that one step further, thinking that women make the same judgment.

The initial step for Brad is to admit he doesn't feel right faking it all the time, as the man did above. The next step is to realize you can't know how other people feel — unless you ask them.

For women, the task is a little trickier. They must attempt to set the stage for discussion. Easier said than done. But a good bet is to set time aside on a weekend when the worries of the work place are not so pervasive. It's also helpful to ease into the idea by expressing your feelings on the subject. Avoid creating the feeling of a test. Ten points for the right answer — no goodies if you guess wrong.

Perhaps the most important point is not to give up if the first attempt fails. You are dealing with someone who believes that expressing feelings is dangerous. If he cried on the playground, he got teased mercilessly, or worse, beat up. That early training is a powerful force to try to defuse. It may take a long time for him to trust the idea of sharing. You may only reap bits and pieces at a time and have to weave the whole picture together for yourself. But that is progress. That's where it all begins.

CHAPTER TWO

THE CODE DEFINED

Question for men: Do you often feel as if you are walking through life with a mask on, pretending to conform to a masculine ideal?

As a boy travels down the long road to manhood, he is repeatedly reminded of what it means to be a man. To be a man basically means three things: achieve, achieve, and achieve some more. To be "adequate" is an insult. Mediocrity is for losers. And any past accomplishments are ancient history, as each day brings a new test of manhood. One fellow journalist, in describing his professional pressure, puts it well: "You're only as good as your last by-line."

Women certainly have the same pressures and many that are uniquely theirs. But as we will explore later, women generally develop other parts of their lives beyond their career — whereas men often do not.

Being a man means being strong in the face of any storm. This is a truly Herculean endeavor that leaves little time for silly things such as understanding or worrying about being understood.

The haunting of the male begins with these role expectations that are programmed into him at a tender age. From the first blue or pink robes that are put on us when we enter this world, our early experiences weave a very different emotional tapestry. By early adulthood a man is on his way into a well of loneliness, while often the women in his life wonder why he's so insensitive and unapproachable.

Waking up

A man in his thirties and beyond will often wake up and not even know why he feels compelled to do certain things. He doesn't know why, for instance, he is jockeying for a promotion when he hates his work. He doesn't know why he is devastated when his secretary simply mentions his growing paunch. He doesn't know why his wife claims that he's resistant to change or doesn't spend enough time with the children, when he's devoted himself to making good money so they can have everything they want.

He doesn't know why his muscles twitch every time he thinks about his bank account or investment portfolio, even though he's already worth more than he ever dreamed possible. He is driven, but he's not sure who is doing the driving, or where he is going. In sum, he doesn't know why "enough is never enough."

When he wakes up in a cold sweat, he wonders, "What's wrong with me?"

We're not talking wimps here; we're talking mainstream men, the fast-track corporate executive, the calm, cool quarterback. He can embody the American dream — and often does.

But real men don't eat quiche and real men don't get afraid, so these haunted feelings are silly and not to be dwelled upon. Dirty Harry never asks for help.

A perilous survival manual

Although the rules have never been written down, I have yet to meet a man who didn't *know* The Code. It's much like the specter of *The Right Stuff* that Tom Wolfe wrote about when dealing with pilots and astronauts. No one talked about The Code or wrote about it. And no one could pin it down in so many words . . . but it was there. A pilot either had "the right stuff" or he didn't. If he didn't, you might feel sorry for him, but he was no good for your partner.

Even men who have never thought about The Code on a conscious level live under it. In fact, most women sense The Code exists. Many women have told me that they feel each man is given a book sometime during his formative years. A man memorizes the rules and then the book disappears, never to be seen by outsiders. And in a sense, they're right. The Code represents a survival manual of sorts, passed down in an unspoken language from generation to generation.

The basic tenets of The Code are simple, embodying the masculine model for appropriate behavior:

Compete and win

All other men are competitors (threats)

Be confident

Be silent

Be strong

Talk is cheap — actions pack clout

Know your turf — and defend it

Don't talk feelings, talk facts

Play (or work) hurts

Hold the upper hand in all relationships

Never let them see you sweat

The more power, the better

Women will love and esteem you in direct proportion to your success

Women want performance — in and out of bed

Women don't really understand the rules men play by

You understand hardball and are willing to play it

Children want fathers they can admire

Be your own man

Work defines worth

Don't hang around with losers — sympathy is for wimps

Be an enigma — never reveal your private thoughts.

And each of these rules contains it's own list of subtexts. For example, part of the silent rule includes never expressing a range of emotions, particularly when it comes to telling a woman you love her. Sound like a couple of dozen John Wayne or Clint Eastwood movies?

While we are on the subject of women, The Code says a man must *always* be ready and willing for sex. Make a move for it, even if in your heart you really don't want to. Performance is key. Yet, the ever-ready stud is a myth, as many women are well aware.

The Real Man Model scorns all effeminate behavior, to the point of hating "queers." And he would rather be dead than to be labeled, even wrongfully labeled, a failure.

It's also important to point out that there are positive aspects to The Code. Your word is your bond. You always take care of your own. Sometimes a little Dirty Harry is needed to pull through a tight spot.

And there is the fine print of The Code. It's hard to determine if these are "good" or "bad" aspects. Many times they reflect double messages. For example: Settle down with a competent woman (but one whose achievements don't overshadow your own). Relate and play with your children (but never let them see you anxious or afraid). Try to achieve more than the previous generation, than your father, (but win his love in the process).

The fine print also translates into the good old performance equals lovability equation. Absolutely no math experience is needed for this one. Every male knows it by heart. The greater your achievements (performances), the more deserving you are of being loved. Catch the winning touchdown pass and your date with the cute cheerleader is in the bag. Drop it — and you know the rest.

Unfortunately, the more a man's performance anxiety escalates, the less able he is to perform well. But hey — Dirty Harry never flinched when pulling the trigger, right?

Programmed to fail

While men like to think of themselves as the rational sex, they continue to live their lives by these unreal, irrational mandates. Many aspects of The Code are not only inappropriate but deadly. They may have made sense in the past when saber-toothed tigers were the enemy instead of the IRS and car payments, but in today's world it is, for the most part, harmful to men and those who love them.

Centuries of macho myths and expectations have created men who are programmed to fail emotionally. Often in middle age, if not before, the lovable, boyish, successful male becomes an unfunny, fatal joke.

Today, the male's traditional way of dealing with life is regularly ridiculed in books and encounter groups, while Hollywood and Marlboro ads propagate the myth. Men are also receiving mixed messages from the "new woman," which often cause them to retreat even more into the pseudo-safety of the structure of The Code.

Differences caused by The Code

Because of The Code, men and women often have very different responses to the same events or circumstances. The following example illustrates my point:

Marie and John, who have been married for fourteen years, decide to take a late night trip to a shopping mall in another part of the city. They stroll to opposite ends of the mall to conduct their shopping.

Marie spies Jerry, the husband of her close friend and bridge partner, Babs, walking arm-in-arm with a bubbly bimbo into a lingerie store. When they emerge with packages in hand, she carefully follows them through the maze of stores, recording every kiss and giggle.

At the other end of the mall, John walks into a lounge and orders a drink before he sees Gloria, his best friend Harold's wife, holding hands with her boss at a dimly lit table. He quickly gulps down his Cutty and water and rushes out of the mall to stand in the rain and think.

On the way home, Marie is angry and animated as she recounts her discovery to her husband. Marie goes on to say that as soon as Jerry left the mall, she found a pay phone and informed Babs of what her philandering husband was up to.

John is silent.

The next day John plays eighteen holes of golf and drinks two six-packs of beer with Harold, as they had previously scheduled, talking about the Lakers, the price of gold, and what a cute ass the new waitress at the club has. John never mentions what he saw last night. Why? The Code.

Marie's first thought had been to tell her friend the truth, no matter how painful it might be. Her system of internal checks and balances told her that it was better for Babs to know what was going on immediately.

Regardless of John's first instinct, The Code dictated silence. Why cause his friend pain? It would only humiliate him. He would be embarrassed if he knew John knew. This is information better kept to himself.

The cost of The Code

Unfortunately, even when a man catches a glimpse of his true self, he discounts it by telling himself: "It's supposed to be this way. Other guys face the same situation and *like* it." And even worse, he tries to convince himself that nothing is wrong. He hears the voice of "reason" telling him, "Face it. Face it, and like it. Because if you don't, you won't be *a man*. And you should die rather than not be a real man."

And die men do. If you think I'm being melodramatic, talk to a life insurance salesman about the American male's mortality risks. Suicide, heart disease, most forms of cancer, homicide, accidental death, drug- and alcohol-related death — you name it — men die from it at a significantly higher rate than women do.[1]

If you look at the latest *Statistical Abstract of the United States,* published in 1990, the differences are astonishing. The 1986 statistics for death rates from heart disease are a case in point. For men, age twenty-five to thirty-four years old, 11.8 per 100,000 in population die due to heart disease. By comparison, 5.5 females (per 100,000 population) die as a result of heart disease. By the time males hit the age range of fifty-five to sixty-four years, the rate per 100,000 population is 627.1; for females in the same age bracket, the rate is 244.1.[2]

The number of men who die from cirrhosis of the liver, which is commonly caused by alcoholism, is nearly twice the number of women for all age groups. In 1986, for the age group of fifty-five to sixty-four years of age, 4,700 men died due to chronic liver disease, versus 2,400 women.[3]

It starts from the time of birth and continues, as numbers from the United States National Center for Health Statistics confirm. For male babies under one year old in 1987, there were

1,129 who died per 100,000 in population in the United States. The death rate for female babies under one year was 902 per 100,000 in population. By the time males and females reach the age bracket of fifteen to twenty-four, males are dying at a rate three times higher than females.[4]

The trend continues. At almost all age levels thereafter, the male death rate is at least 100 percent higher.[5] A man's world indeed!

By the time men reach their seventies, those who make it, they are committing suicide at a rate roughly eight times greater than women.[6] While more women attempt suicide, their failure rate may mean they view it as a desperate vehicle to reach out to family and friends. Men rarely issue such warnings. When they fall on the sword, they make sure to get it right. Men typically use a more violent means to kill themselves, such as guns.

Without a doubt, there are physiological and genetic differences in the sexes, which account for some of the higher mortality risks. For now, we can have little influence over the genetic risks. It's from birth on that we can affect men's lives for the better.

How? First, we can recognize the many rationalizations that can cause The Code to remain ingrained. These include:

• If people don't really know you, they can't see your weak points. Therefore, you strive to present an enigma that hides your flaws.

• Others will love you if you always appear strong.

• People will look to you for answers (and respect you) because there never seems to be a problem that you can't handle.

• Everyone is counting on you. You don't have time to have a bad day or the luxury to hurt inside.

• You feel safe. As long as you allow no one inside, you are invulnerable (or perceive yourself to be).

- You have a sense of belonging in the "world of men."

- You think the only good man is a "useful" man. Nobody wants the weak guy on his team, so you know you've got to make the cut, and you'll do what it takes to get there.

- Change doesn't represent opportunity; it represents risk. You preserve the *status quo* (The Code) to the greatest extent possible because it offers comfort and security.

Breaking out

What a man needs to hear is that he that he doesn't have to buy into this. If he does buy into it, he gets caught up in a vicious cycle of emotional denial. Outwardly, he appears friendly, confident, and eager to fit the male expectations. But his haunted insides begin to rot. Living under the spell of The Code represents a serious denial of true feelings.

A man must also learn to listen to his own inner voice, that not-so-gentle nudge reminding him of his own humanity, his frailties, his compassion.

But men's behavior will change most dramatically when they no longer feel rewarded for living by The Code. The answer to breaking The Code is for men and women to change their approval criteria.

Whether they recognize it or not, women exert tremendous power over the behavior of men. Men influence women's behavior as well but inevitably, both sexes posture and pose for each other. But we often pay the price by ending up as caricatures of ourselves.

Men are Pavlovian enough that they will do what it takes to get the reward. And the reward for men is achieving the respect of men and the admiration of women.

In other words, if a macho man finds his behavior gets him laughed at instead of cooed over, he'll stop immediately. If a man thinks his Code-like behavior is perceived as silly, and he becomes the butt of jokes, he'll adjust and fast.

All too often, women try to solve the problem with blunt criticism. It happens all the time, in the office and where the home fires are burning. The problem is that criticizing macho behavior typically has the reverse effect: it makes the man more defensive and more into his tough-guy act. The following letter illustrates the point:

Dear Dr. Towery:

I don't classify myself as a rabid feminist, but when I feel I am being treated in a sexist fashion at work I say something. I try a straightforward approach, and tell the guys when their behavior is inappropriate.

I thought my fellow male managers in the department would appreciate it. I know I'd want someone to tell me if I was acting in an offensive way and not aware of it. Not true. All I see is them acting really defensive around me and literally walking out of a room when I come in. I'm confused. What's all this about men liking a straightforward approach, no BS? How can I get things back on track?

Let's look at how women today affect male behavior. Many men walk around in a state of confusion. They fear being labeled a "chauvinist" by women. On the other hand, they have difficulty deciphering what it is women really want. Is opening a door for a business associate proper etiquette and politeness, or a condescending "power gesture"?

The truth is, men do fear angry feminists because they don't know how to deal with them. They don't know how to diffuse the anger. It feels so omnipresent — directed at all men — and it appears impossible for one man to be able to change the situation.

While I understand women's anger at sexist behavior, retaliated hate isn't the answer. Anger causes men to first retreat and then regroup with renewed vigor.

Women tend to give mixed signals to men. What do I mean?

If women say they want the "new man" with sensitivity, they need to vote with their hearts. "Why is it," one male nurse asked me, "that these same female nurses who complain about the cold, arrogant doctors seem to swoon when the jerks walk into the room? They bitch constantly about 'money-mad, power-hungry, controlling doctors,' but will drop everything to be able to go out with one."

The problem men face is sifting through double messages. If female nurses, as an example, dislike being ordered around by arrogant, chauvinistic doctors, why are they in any way attracted to them? If the female nurses truly value sensitive men, they should date male nurses. But male nurses report that they are generally snubbed for the doctors because of the doctors' status and wallets. The point is, when and if the female nurses send a message to arrogant, pushy doctors that their behavior is disgusting — and that they are fed up with it and them — then they will change. And surprisingly fast.

Everybody wants to be accepted. Most of us are even crazy enough to want to be liked. So, if a man finds himself on the outside looking in, he is going to figure out how to change the situation. If women truly are fed up with men's insensitivity, inaccessibility, etc., the beauty is that they, to a large extent, hold the keys to change.

A man's driving need is for acceptance and approval from the fairer sex. When women identify Code-like behavior as inappropriate, without a doubt, men will change.

Easing up

Am I some sort of male apologist, trying to say everything's up to women? And that they, and they alone, have put us in this predicament to begin with?

No!

But just as the women's movement recognized that part of what needed to be done was to change women's perceptions about themselves and change men's perceptions of them, so too does breaking out of The Code involve both sexes. If women want men to alter their macho behavior, they need to understand that there are chains that hold men in place. They can ridicule the situation, but if they really want to see change, they need to become involved in easing things up.

When the weight is never removed from a man's shoulders, he begins to feel powerless, and like a wounded animal, he strikes out. It's the age-old masculine way of controlling his environment.

I know several intelligent, well-reared men who occasionally tell the most outlandishly offensive jokes against women that I've ever had the displeasure to hear. I'm not saying they shouldn't be condemned for this — there's no excuse. But knowing them and realizing that these jokes are based on fear and anger is the first step toward helping them to stop. Anger is the typical male response to feeling helpless, whether in the personal or professional realm. As one reader wrote in concerning his work:

Dear Dr. Towery:

My boss has made some decisions over the last two years that I think are wrecking our company. I'm powerless to stop him or have any real influence over him. As a result of his incompetence I'm getting no raise, no bonus and eventually may have no job. I am so mad at him I feel like I'm going to bust a gut. I don't sleep well, eat well, like sex or anything else that I used to enjoy. How can I deal with this anger?

All of us tend to become angry when we have no choice or option. Women often seem to be more talented at handling helplessness and anger by expressing them outwardly and getting it out of their system with friends. This man has a sense of powerlessness that is going to manifest itself one way or another against his boss or job.

In a work situation, such as the one above, it is possible to stay. But it is important to keep in mind that your work is only one part of the total equation that equals you. While you can't control your work, you can enjoy and control other, equally important areas of your life.

This same principle applies to personal relationships also. As we have seen, many men feel trained to behave a certain way, usually the Code way, and then feel vilified when they do.

If a woman wants to change certain behavior, she can best do this not by bringing the negative behavior constantly into focus, but instead concentrating on the more agreeable options. Flattery works better than criticism. Present positive ways for him to change. Talk about the solutions, not just the problems.

In a workshop I conducted, one woman said her husband could never get home to dinner on time. As she told me:

If I said I was going to serve dinner at 6:00 p.m., he would come home at 6:30. If I said, okay, let's have dinner at 7:00, he would walk in the door at 7:30 p.m. There didn't seem to be an explanation other than the fact that he was a rude person who didn't care about eating dinner with his wife and children.

I recommended she schedule a dinner for Monday, Wednesday and Friday, but let him "fend for himself" on Tuesdays and Thursdays. She confessed to feeling skeptical about the schedule, but agreed to try it. A month into the new schedule, she wrote me a brief note:

I thought I would let you know that my husband is doing pretty well on Mondays, Wednesdays, and Fridays. Not perfect — but close. The interesting thing is he finally told me why he was always late for dinner. Evidently, his mother always served breakfast at 6:30 a.m. and dinner at 6:30 p.m. and he had to eat everything on his plate. He came to hate the routine and was still in the process of rebelling.

It was nice to finally talk about it, and to not feel so personally affronted by his chronic lateness. Now, he says, he doesn't feel so hemmed in. Thanks for a simple solution.

Not all problems are so simple to solve. But many are easier than we first suspect. The important thing is to try to come up with ideas for compromise and to begin a dialogue.

Anger and accusations bring out the worst in everyone, perhaps more so in men than women. For men, anger is often suppressed, or even repressed, until it explodes in an oblique, possibly violent manner. Women are typically more direct with their emotions. Yet, solutions rarely come to light in the heat of an argument or bitter feud.

Before getting caught up in anger, it is critical to look for a way out and then talk about it. It sounds all too simple, but it is important. Psychotherapists now agree that anger is one of the most misunderstood of all emotions.

If you recall, the sixties was the decade of "letting it all hang out." Out of that came the notion that expressing anger was healthier. If you let it out, you would live longer — or so the myth went.

Studies prove it is a myth, as Carol Tavris points out in her book, *Anger: The Misunderstood Emotion*. Tavris analyzed the work of the Western Collaborative Group Study, which has followed 3,154 men, aged thirty-nine to fifty-nine for years to see which of them develop coronary heart disease. According to the study, the Type A personality, who is achievement-driven and feels impatient much of the time, is at risk for heart disease. But the men at risk of illness were also those who directed their anger outward and were likely to become angry more than once a week.[7]

A second study in Massachusetts, however, yielded different results. Yes, Type-A personalities were more at risk for heart disease. But so too were the men who suppressed their anger.[8]

So are we supposed to ventilate our anger or suppress it? It seems like we lose no matter what we do. No we don't, says Tavris. What is important is to see anger as a symptom of what else is going on in our lives and not as a cause in itself. If we are going to be social creatures, we cannot always express our anger. And suppressed anger is not likely to have medical consequences, Tavris says, "if we feel in control of the situation that is causing the anger, if we interpret the anger as a sign of a grievance to be corrected instead of as an emotion to be sullenly protected. . . ."[9]

It is important to recognize that anger is not an isolated emotion. There are other emotions at play. If a woman is furious with her spouse for coming home late every night, she must realize that she is filled with not only anger. Her self-esteem is probably hurt and she may be dealing with a fear of abandonment.

Our anger also has a purpose. It makes a grievance known. If the grievance is not confronted, it won't matter whether the anger is kept inside or let out.

As cognitive therapists now reinforce, each person needs to realize that another human being has a unique internal script. It is a script that colors all of his or her emotions and reactions to situations.

For men, The Code is a major chunk of their internal message center. It benefits no one to deny its existence. By the same token, women have their own script. And added to that are the personal variations created during our childhoods.

Take Mary Ellen, a woman who came to one of my workshops while her divorce was pending. Looking at her past for patterns, she realized that her mother and her younger sister were "best friends." In her words, "They were more alike. It was only natural for them to be together, doing the same things they both loved whether it was gardening or shopping."

Yet, Mary Ellen had grown up with a strong sense of "being number two." She was overly sensitive to words that sounded "maybe critical." Every time her husband said he admired another woman for her ability to negotiate deals or whatever, Mary Ellen was signing her divorce papers in her head. She was going to get out before he abandoned her for someone else.

Just knowing this pattern helped her to throw new light on many of her interactions with people — not just her husband, but people at work, or friends in the neighborhood. Did the knowledge save the marriage? That remains to be seen. But at least she doesn't have to color people's thoughts concerning her with a gray crayon left over from childhood.

CHAPTER THREE

SOCIETY'S ROLE AND THE CODE

Question for men: Do you remember learning early on that real men are willing to stand alone and like it?

Before continuing to discuss various ways to move beyond The Code, it is important to analyze the early messages boys receive that ingrain The Code. These early messages, given in the celebrated formative years, stay forever. It helps to understand how much effort is involved in a man breaking The Code when we understand how he got the messages in the first place.

The Dawning of The Code

I'm not sure when it first dawned on me that there was a Code. I'm not even sure when I started learning the rules.

It could have been when the nurse in the hospital nursery picked up the crying little girl in the crib next to mine, inundating her with goo-goo tickles, while casting a disapproving frown at my squalling face?

Or was it when I stuck my cousin, who was four years my elder, with the handle of a rake and subsequently had my head crammed in a pile of cow manure in the barnyard? He had been bossing me around and making me do more work than I thought appropriate for my tender years, so I figured I could give him a jab, make my point, and get away unscathed. Wrong.

Even though I was technically the guilty party, there was no doubt in my mind that my uncle would have punished my cousin's worthless hide, if I had just told the truth about what had happened. After all, at fourteen, he was considered a young man, and should have been tolerant of one who had just turned ten. Or at least not go and stick his head in cow manure, an extremely unpleasant experience, I assure you. Even though I hated my cousin's guts at that moment, no way was I going to tattle. The Code was in place.

Isn't that what real men do?

Nuances of The Code are everywhere for young boys. I can remember hiding in the theater after the kiddie matinee was over to watch the adult's movies and see how big people behaved. I winced in pain as the corrupt union leaders beat Marlon Brando senseless in *On the Waterfront*. Enduring his pain stoically, he then staggered past the incredulous thugs, somehow making it alone, without anyone's help, so his buddies could now be free from tyranny. He was the perfect male role model.

I think my favorite, however, was Gary Cooper in *High Noon*. Now there was a man. Not even the astoundingly beautiful Grace Kelly could lure him from fighting to the death the murderous pack of outlaws who were out to do him in. And when the townsmen turned out to be cowards and wouldn't help, he did it alone. This is the ultimate male fantasy trip: Whipping the world's ass alone. And then being loved for it.

Beyond those early instructions from Hollywood on appropriate male behavior, I have other strong childhood memories. Memories that served to enforce The Code. The following is an excerpt from my personal journal, which I started much later in life:

The grizzled, weather-parched men in faded overalls and brogan shoes were yelling, cursing, and handing money back and forth to each other. "What are you doing, Jim — what's going on?" I wheezed, as the older men encircled us.

"Fight me with all you've got," my young cousin whispered, "or we're in deep shit."

The grimy dirt was suddenly in my ears and nose, with sweat — mine and his — stinging my eyes. My cousin, with whom I had been singing "When Johnny Comes Marching Home" with just minutes ago, was trying to get his forearm between my chin and collarbone — in other words, choke me.

"You're kidding . . ." I began as his left fist caught me in the ear and just as an old man's tobacco juice splattered my face. But it was my cousin's desperate look that forced me to kick him with my free right foot, causing his head to crash forward into mine. As our heads locked in the sweat and blood between us, he said: "Fight hard, dammit!"

And fight we did, until thank God, I caught a glimpse of my daddy heading toward us in a battered pickup truck. The old men scattered, saying "Mr. Clarence is here. All bets off."

My Daddy never asked what had happened; he knew. He had grown up, I found out later, with the same rituals until he had been crippled from a horse accident. He put us in the truck and for the first and only time in my life peeled rubber.

My cousin said they pitted young boys against each other all the time and called the loser a "pussy," a new word to me. Of course the word would later come to play a prominent role in my life, along with "queer," "wimp," "baby," "coward," "sissy," and many others.

Jim started crying and as I looked at my cousin who had just finished choking me a few minutes ago, I remember thinking, "Something really strange is going on here."

The rest of my life taught me I was more right than I ever could have known at the time. My cousin and I were well along the way to being haunted by The Code.

Society's role

The English comedy group Monty Python has a running gag in which some poor sap commits the most incredible and hilarious crimes imaginable and then offers up that it's "all society's fault."

One can certainly take the ambiguous "society's" role too far, but society does play a significant role in developing the haunted male. The smallest gestures eventually have a ripple effect. Little girl babies are put in a pink or feminine blanket, little boys in a blue one. We don't want any pink-suited sissies out there.

Although studies show that male infants are touched more, female infants are talked to and smiled at more often. Even female vocalizations are imitated more by adults, though male infants vocalize as much. And parents spend more time encouraging females to smile or to vocalize.[10]

As babies grow from infancy, little girls are held more often when they cry, while the little boy is left to "tough it out," and later told to "grow up and act like a little man." At three years old? Sure. Don't want to start any bad habits, like depending on others for emotional support, or learning to release fear to enjoy comfort. Silly human things like that.

The messages we give little boys are clear: "Hold back those tears. Stand up for yourself and pop that bully in the nose if he ever steals another toy from you." Conversely, we tell little girls to report similar incidents to the teacher — the intrinsically sensible thing to do.

With each outdated message we insert one more piece of the mosaic that will become the ghost to haunt him the rest of his life. Crazily enough, it ends up haunting the women in his life as well, for they can't understand his "craziness," or his lack of communication.

Lessons learned

A respected psychologist, Patricia H. Arnold, gives us a revealing message that boys begin to receive by nursery school. Dr. Arnold, who teaches organizational behavior and theory courses at Vanderbilt University in Nashville, Tennessee, refers to a study conducted in the late seventies.

Observers were sent into nursery school classrooms to see whether the teachers (all female) treated little boys and girls differently. She identifies the results as one of the reasons boys seem to become self-reliant (a personality trait with good and bad aspects) at an early age.

While the teachers denied that they differentiated in any way, the study painted another picture altogether. There were dramatic differences. When the boys requested help, for example, they were given detailed verbal instructions on how to do the project themselves. When girls requested help, they were encouraged to hang around, and wait until the teacher was free. In many cases, the teachers would not only directly assist the girls, but do the project for them.

The researchers found this pattern occurring over and over again, whether in the science corner or the housekeeping corner. If the kids were in the kitchen making applesauce, and a boy needed help, he was given more information about how to do it himself, and the clear message: "You can do this, and I expect you to. Go off and do it. If you need information, come back."

By comparison, little girls receive a clearer message that they need to get other people to not only like them, but to help them. The message for them, Dr. Arnold notes, is: "Honey, you're cute and you're sweet and I love you. If you can't quite handle this by yourself right now, just hang around and I'll help you when I'm finished."

Throughout the early years and into adulthood, men are repeatedly given a different message: "You can do it. You're a man." The troubling aspect of this is that the converse of that message is very readily apparent to boys and young men struggling with their manhood: "If you can't do it, you are not a man." Failure, cowardice, the whole notion of being a "pussy" enter his vocabulary at an early age. These seeds are planted and then carefully nurtured for a performance orientation.

At a time when women are openly resisting time-honored roles they find limiting, men trot out without so much as a whimper to receive their eventual early demise. Herb Goldberg notes in his book, *The Hazards of Being Male: Surviving the Myth of Masculine Privilege,* that too many men continue to act as if they can stand up under, and even enjoy, all the expectations placed on their shoulders. And it doesn't matter how contradictory the expectations are, or how adverse the consequences.[11]

Thank goodness the women's movement helped women challenge their obsolete and restricting roles. Now it's men's turn.

Reasonable expectations

Syndicated columnist Ellen Goodman is well-known for identifying the plight of the "First World" women of America. By simply adding new expectations to the old ones, Goodman suggests that women are fueling a "Superdrudge Syndrome" for themselves.

I think the same applies to men. Men are beginning to feel guilty if they don't fulfill the old roles *and* the new ones — many of which are contradictory. In a public appearance in Nashville, Tennessee, Goodman once said that the demand for men is to be Superman: "A man is now supposed to be open, caring, supportive, able to leap tall emotional buildings in one bound and become vice president of General Motors at the same time."

Men are caught between the dual expectations of being cold and calculating enough to be pitted against the toughest corporate wolves and then being a thoughtful and sensitive lover or parent.

Goodman is right. It is impossible to pile on new role demands without taking care of some of the old ones. Just as women need to take the best of the traditional and merge it with new possibilities, men must recognize the need for shedding the limitations of the old-style roles to reach new goals. A sane balance is necessary.

"The new demand for men," Goodman quipped, "is to be a wonderful combination of John Wayne, Alan Alda and Bruce Springsteen, or a new kind of muscular sensitive." Nice work if you can get it. Unfortunately, most of us, being human, can't manage it — at least not all the time.

People are like vessels. If we are full of the old expectations, there is nowhere to put the new ones. In order for the new healthy ways to grow, we have to let go of some of the old, unhealthy ones.

Out of the woods

Change will be slow. Bringing up a "liberated" boy, for example, isn't easy. Elizabeth Stone wrote an incredibly humorous editorial for *Savvy* magazine on the pitfalls of raising a son. Having made a vow as a feminist mother to never bring home militaristic toys, such as guns, swords or tanks, she found her son had other ideas. In her words: "We never taught him the word 'gun,' but when he got to feel at home with syntax and suffixes, he requested a 'shoot-er.' "[12] It was the first of many hints that theory and practice aren't necessarily bedfellows.

For another feminist mother, Stone says, the light came on when her son propped up a copy of a *Peter, Paul and Mary* album, making it a fortress that he could crouch behind and shoot from. "That's an album, not a fortress," she wailed. "I *know* that," the little guy shot back. At times like these, Stone continues, "one's enlightened approach to son-raising seems a mere pebble facing a tidal wave of genes and/or culture."[13]

The fact that her son developed a shelf full of army equipment, Superman costumes, and guns, however, was not exactly an accident, Stone confides. "I allowed them to happen because, in short, I wanted my son to be at home with Boy Culture. And little boys do have one, which is separate from play."[14]

Yet, it isn't all downhill by any means. Stone laughed when her five-year-old son taught his one-year-old brother how to make the *"bukhew"* noise of gunshot and to point his stubby finger "just so." But, she has also heard him soothingly croon to stop his brother from crying. As she puts it: "My younger son's wails ebbed as his brother continued to croon to him. And it was like hearing the light at the end of the tunnel."[15]

While there is more hope for the next generation, there are also specific actions a man can take to move out of the limitations of The Code. After recognizing that The Code is, in effect, a decaying forest, he can see his way clear with suggestions such as the following:

- Every time you catch yourself playing the perfect, unconquerable hero, jot the instance down in a personal diary or notebook. Ask yourself who it is that benefited from your tough-guy stance. Who is it that you have to impress? And what did you give up in return? Intimacy? Honesty? Test your own perceived gain. You may be giving up more than you realize.

- List your fears. That's right, your fears. It might not be easy at first to even admit you have any. But articulating what scares you, even just to yourself, is helpful. Look at what you've written and realize that you can disarm every one of those fears, one way or another.

- Tell your wife or partner that you are tired of the "macho tough mode," and you would like her to help you see your way clear of it. Make it a game. Learn to laugh at yourself when you slip up. Adding humor to the situation does wonders at lightening up the darker side of this type of behavior.

- On a day-to-day basis, try making statements about how you feel, rather than statements about last night's game or the current status of your car. Go easy at first. Accept the fact straight off that not everyone is dying to hear about your feelings. Just don't let the response of others be your excuse for keeping it all inside.

- Know what you are good at, and value it. Take some pride and satisfaction in it. Everyone is so good at telling you how and when you mess up that you've probably become pretty good at the same thing. Balance it. Become good at recognizing when you make good.

- Opening up doesn't mean confessing every lousy deed you ever committed, or harping about how you've been shafted by others. That's dumping, not sharing. That can make you feel worse than when you started.

- Finally, be true to yourself — not to The Code. You owe it nothing. Practice being honest with yourself at all times, especially when you're having trouble talking with others.

CHAPTER FOUR

RELATIONSHIP ROULETTE

Question for women: Do you feel the pressure to achieve, yet feel that too much success translates into relationship roulette?

In my preliminary research for this book, I was struck by how many women think their success alienates men. I was also surprised by how little has been written about how men really feel about successful women in either the professional or personal realm.

From the woman's perspective, however, there is a lot of speculating, especially in women's magazines. Essentially, there is a lingering suspicion among women that to achieve any form of measurable success means playing relationship roulette.

A random sampling of women's publications, particularly those that target career-oriented women, reinforces that how men respond to women's achievements remains an important issue. Looking back, for example, a cover line from the March 1986 issue of *New Woman* reads: "When Couples Compete: Can You Be Lovers and Rivals?"[16] Similarly, an article by Dr. Harriet B. Braiker in the January 1987 issue of *Working Woman* asks: "Who Is the Right Man for a Woman Like You?"[17] Braiker is referring to top achievers. Again, a cover line for the July 1988 issue of *Cosmopolitan* reads: "When You're Smarter than He Is."[18]

Much of this speculating centers on the question: How can a woman enjoy success and the power it brings without stomping on her man's fragile ego?

There's no one answer. Many men can handle a woman's success, even if it eclipses their own; many men cannot. "In order to deal with the issue effectively," suggests a management consultant I interviewed, "it will take men openly talking about how they would feel about their wife hauling in more money than they do."

She's right. Too often what we see now are attitudes or postures, not real feelings. And we see them from both sides. We still hear sexist jokes from men — such as disparaging references to female managers "being on the rag."

In all fairness, we hear the same remarks from women, such as, "You better sidestep Pam today. She has PMS." Or, we hear successful single women attributing their failure to find partners to their high-powered careers. We even see new labels for dual-career couples coming from the media, such as "DINS," short for "double income, no sex."

Why are men so nervous?

The reason *men* are nervous is clear. This is treacherous ground if you were brought up to assume a woman would love you *and* be dependent on you both for support and status. The Code teaches men that they are the stronger sex. They are the protectors. And traditionally, the adult male demonstrated his love to a woman through making a living for her and the family. It goes beyond the simplistic idea of "that's just something a man does," because it's his way of expressing his commitment.

As many married women have discovered, it's easier for a man to hand his wife a check for next month's groceries than a simple note that says, "I love you."

The reason men — and women — are nervous about women's success hinges on deeply ingrained role expectations, and there is no quick fix to remedy all of the different issues that play a part. First, almost all of us grew up with the expectation that the proper role of the male is to be a good provider; the female's income has been viewed by and large as supplemental. The male ego, his self-image, is heavily invested in how many dollars *he* brings home. This is unfortunate, but true.

Status/Money/Intelligence

It is important to point out that there are three separate issues involved with a woman's success as it impacts her relationship with a man: (1) her career status; (2) the amount of money she brings home; and (3) her basic intelligence. Before progressing any further, let me say that mature men can handle a large income from their wives — even enjoy the freedom it brings them. Many men can also appreciate a woman who has achieved exceptional career status. However, if a woman is innately smarter than the man she is with, and both are aware of the fact, it seems to bode ill for the future of the relationship.

In this latter category, I am not referring to the women who are married to men like Albert Einstein. Einstein, for all his brilliant theories, was not able to find his way home, literally, and on several occasions reportedly asked policemen to help him find his address. In other words, these are men who are extremely talented in one area, but limited or at least average in others. What I am referring to are relationships in which the woman is constantly having to cover for her partner's lack of intelligence in a broad range of categories. The woman's embarrassment, in this case, is only rivaled by her boredom.

From the male perspective, it also becomes a painful source of embarrassment. Although a lot of men give lip service to the notion that "a woman can't be too smart for me," in reality, most men are uncomfortable if they continually come up short in brainpower. It certainly doesn't sit well, according to The Code. If one were able to sift through the source of many of the most explosive arguments in relationships, a central source would be when men feel "dumb."

Julie, a young stockbroker, shares an excellent example:

When I was growing up, I remember my Dad making one bad investment after another. It was like he was jinxed. I used to feel sorry for him, because every time he and my Mom had an argument she would berate him for his stupid investments.

The results were always predictable. My Dad is one of those who when they get mad, their voice gets quieter and quieter, not louder, until it explodes. He would try to withdraw and ignore my Mom for about fifteen or twenty minutes, but she would keep after him until he just exploded. It's funny, when he started into his rages, I don't even remember what he was saying. I just remember my Mom running for cover, and that would be the end of it.

The status duel

While status clashes can present a problem, they can also be resolved in a healthy relationship. It's not so much a question of how different the couple is in terms of status, but how well they are able to communicate on those differences. A TV anchor woman, for example, might be married to a stock analyst for a small, local firm. Her more visible success could become an issue if the couple refused to address it. In such situations, it is important to isolate the real issue, particularly when quarrels overtly begin for other reasons.

Both partners must also be able to look objectively at the judgments other people form. Superstar Cher once became involved with a bagel maker twenty years her junior. The status difference between the two drew public attention. In fact, Cher was asked during an interview with Barbara Walters if she would be willing to marry the young man, and if so, how did she *feel* about it. Without reservation, Cher said, "Yes, I would," but the young man was not willing to marry her. It was a question that would never have been asked if Cher were involved with an older, wealthy man. To her credit, Cher (and other women like her) have established a reputation for being able to isolate what qualities are really important to her, and then acting on them — regardless of the general public's opinion.

Hitting the problem head-on

One of the easiest ways to resolve status clashes is to address them head-on. Although many people want a quick fix, there is no magic formula. One woman, who is a well-known model, wrote to ask for "a method" to deal with her boyfriend's inability to accept her fame.

Dear Dr. Towery:

What do you do if you are with an otherwise super guy who gets mad when people refer to you as "the famous model"? I've been dating Ted for over a year, and it is reaching a point where I'm ready to get out. Every time someone comes up to me at a party and says something about my modeling career, he gets upset. And each time, he seems to get madder and madder. Isn't there a method for handling this?

There are no "easy" methods, but there are simple steps to take. First, put the issue directly on the table. At the same time, sit down and try to figure out if there are other issues that need to be resolved. Often several issues get lumped under one sore spot. Ted, as an example, may be trying to hide a fear of abandonment by making you feel guilty about your status. He may very well be threatened that your recognition will lead to other opportunities — and leave him in the dust.

Once the basics are on the table, agree on a way to "attack" the problem when it surfaces. In other words, the model may simply agree to say, "Ted, you are making me feel guilty again." Oftentimes, each of us develop bad habits and then don't even realize when we are repeating the pattern.

If both people care enough to work at the relationship, progress will be made. It will take time, though. Deep-seated fears don't disappear overnight. My best advice is to stick with it until you are sure you've given it a fair shot. If that doesn't work, at least you have the assurance that you tried.

CHAPTER FIVE

THE MAN'S RESPONSE

Question for men: *Do you consider the achievement-oriented woman a PRIZE or a PIRANHA? Are you really comfortable with a woman's success?*

More than a century ago, Flaubert captured the enigmatic beauty of feminine success:

She [Madame Bovary] had that indefinable beauty that comes from happiness, enthusiasm, success — a beauty that is nothing more or less than a harmony of temperament and circumstances.[19]

But the allure, many high-achieving women discover, seems to come with its own set of drawbacks. Women who achieve a strong measure of success often sense that their partner feels intimidated, or worse, they find it increasingly difficult to attract suitable partners.

Generally speaking, my observation is that men accept successful women in direct proportion to their own success. There is a direct correlation to the man's self-esteem. Men who feel haunted by their own litany of self-doubts, it follows, are not in a position to gracefully accept a woman's accomplishments. This is particularly true if her accomplishments eclipse his own.

The true measure of success

How do Americans define success? In dollars and cents. The hundreds of thousands a professional baseball player makes versus the pocket change that a policeman brings home is hard to justify. "We are in sad times," a real estate marketing executive recently told me, "when we respect a stockbroker who manipulates his way to $250,000 a year over schoolteachers — the people who dedicate themselves to educating the youth of the country — because they make a salary in the mid-twenties."

Real success, he later elaborated during a workshop, means balancing priorities:

I am married to a woman eight years my junior who probably over time will make more money than I. She might want to go back to law school, and I will not stand in her way. One reason I can afford to feel this way is because I know that achievement will not consume her being. I think truly successful people have a priority zone for family and faith values — that ability to balance their lives. It's not a question of how much is on the plate, but how it is balanced.

The one thing the chairman of IBM has in common with the drunk on lower Broad is that they only have twenty-four hours each day. And we each have A, B, C priorities. If your family becomes a C priority, you are not successful. For one thing, your family is going to know your job is more important than they are. You're kidding yourself if you think otherwise. Bottom line is, you won't be considered particularly successful — simply driven.

He hit the nail on the head. Because both men and women have to stop and ask: Success at what cost? Men, in general, are not so much concerned about women's success in the abstract as they are in the specific. They are afraid of emotional, and increasingly, physical desertion. And they feel especially at risk or vulnerable when children are involved. It's not so much a matter of where the woman is heading in her career path, but what is she leaving behind.

Men can easily fall into the trap of "success at all costs." They seem to be better at this than women. A letter I recently received illustrates my point:

Dear Dr. Towery:

I am a senior vice president in a New York Stock Exchange company. I have a good chance of becoming executive vice president within a year. I make over $150,000 a year and own a comfortable home in an exclusive neighborhood. I am thirty-six years old.

I think I have done well for my family for my age. My wife is becoming increasingly less patient with the demands my work places on me. I must work a lot of nights and weekends. My job requires extensive travel. If I don't do it, they will find someone who will. My family lives well: private schools, beach condo, fancy restaurants, you name it.

But my wife keeps wanting me to spend more time with her, talk more and, in general, be what I am not. I don't like to think about divorce but my family doesn't seem to appreciate what I do for them. So I'm starting to wonder what's in it for me.

We are only fooling ourselves if we think that we are living this type of life for the benefit of our families. In the letter above, it seems clear that it is the man who is more interested in the condos and restaurants than his wife; but he does it all in the name of his "family living well."

In such a situation, it's time to stop and reflect where we're trying to go and what we really want. Instead of sacrificing for his family, this guy is sacrificing them — for his career. He's choosing the money over his wife and kids.

It's an easy trap. Many men slowly enter this cave and never come out for light. And men who live by The Code are highly susceptible. It's an easy way to avoid dealing with feelings buried long ago. There's a reason people who spend sixty-plus hours a week at the office are called workaholics. They are addicted to work just as surely as alcoholics are to booze. Work becomes a way to anesthetize their feelings.

As an increasing number of women enter high-powered careers, they too are faced with the same choice. At least the man who wrote in is asking what's wrong. There are far too many people who have been able to combine successful careers with satisfying home lives for the rest of us to rationalize that it just can't be done. To do otherwise is to use your job as a crutch — a way of avoiding intimacy problems. When work overshadows family needs, it's time for a person, man or woman, to stop and reassess personal goals.

The "quality time" myth

I've seen relationships and marriages destroyed by trying to operate on the notion of "quality time." Coming home at 8:30 and trying to reserve thirty minutes of quality time with a child or spouse just doesn't work — whether you are a mother or father. You lose too many of the small, intimate moments that make a family strong.

To build a strong family life takes time and effort. If your daughter wants to tell you about how her teacher was unfair to her, she won't be able to tell you about it tomorrow. It won't be important or remembered tomorrow. But you can bet that it's important today. And as one event folds into the next, one day you may discover that she won't share anything with you anymore.

One woman who dated a traveling salesman pinpoints the problem:

When we first started dating, Jeff was very attentive. He listened to me and made me feel important. For two years I thought I had found the perfect man. Then, he accepted a traveling position with his company. I remember thinking of all the little things that happened on a daily basis that I wanted to talk to him about. But he wasn't there.

When he would come by two or three weeks later, I began noticing that I didn't have anything to say to him. I guess, looking back now, we lost our "intimacy" or whatever. I kept hoping things would change, but when you don't spend time with someone you eventually end up strangers. When I realized how much

he loved being on the road, we broke up. As much as I loved him,
I couldn't face a marriage like that.

While there may be one or two nights a week that you need
to stay at the office, coming home extremely late every night
means you are purposely sacrificing your family life for your
career. It's your choice. But you are only kidding yourself if you
think you can constantly "make it up" to your partner or family.

You are also kidding yourself if you think you aren't making a choice. You are, and the job wins.

CHAPTER SIX

THAT DARNED MONEY MATTER

Questions for women: *Do you view yourself as an equal wage earner in marriage, or do you think of your income as supplemental? Do you think it's dangerous for the woman to be the primary wage earner?*

While money can be a sticky subject between couples, it doesn't have to be. There is a growing trend among singles living together, for example, to simply split the bills. Or, they set up a third, separate account for the purpose of paying bills and share all the couple's joint expenses, regardless of whether one has higher medical bills, child care costs, etc.

In today's world roughly 10 percent of the married women make more than their spouse. That figure is projected to rise as more women enter the labor market and at higher levels. It's also estimated that less than 10 percent of couples today pool all of their financial resources.

The woman's earning power

From the male's perspective, part of the financial difficulties encountered by couples stems from the woman's view of her own earning power. Many times it's women who hesitate to remove themselves from the "second class" wage earner status.

Surely most women believe that they are entitled to equal pay for equal work. But women seem to have difficulty letting go of the notion that their earnings are somehow supplemental. Studies show that the more money a woman makes, the more likely she is to keep it separate from her male partner's money, and the more likely she is to make independent financial decisions.

Both sexes have centuries of conditioning that tell them the male should function as provider. For a number of women, it just doesn't "feel" right to make more money than a man — or to pay half or more of the couple's joint bills. Since finances are such a sensitive issue in a relationship, it's important to be honest about this issue.

Who pays?

Not surprisingly, many men are often confused about the accessibility of women's money. Should he pick up the whole mortgage, but let her pay for the family vacation? Should he pick up the insurance costs, but expect her to pay part of the medical bills? This can lead to a quagmire of financial questions that couples have to face squarely. Trying to skirt money issues or ignore them is a surefire way to end up disappointed or angry.

Ultimately, couples must establish their own sense of what is fair and then learn to trust their partner's willingness to stick to that sense of fairness. The question of who pays for what is a gray area. We don't have role models, or generations of examples of what fair means when there are two paychecks involved. But being on the cutting edge can be exciting. We're setting precedents at a rate never before imagined. We just have to try to set the right ones.

From the male viewpoint

Most men welcome a second income. It alleviates some financial pressures and gives them more latitude to explore career and lifestyle options. More importantly, it relieves them from a debilitating stereotype — that of being a "success object."

The majority of men do not resent the role of provider. It's a time-honored responsibility and one in which they feel comfortable.

But there is a growing number of men, particularly younger men, who do not want to be "landed" like a prize fish. These guys want *partners*, in the real sense of the word, not a dependent woman looking for a rich man to stuff her lizard-skin bag with credit cards. One single business writer in his mid-twenties told me this during a workshop:

I don't see myself as a caretaker. Someday I'll probably leave journalism to make more money. But I can't stand clingy women. I seem to attract more than my fair share. They want me to solve everything. They even want me to solve their girlfriends' problems! I don't know how I get involved in these situations, but I want a woman who is an equal in every way, and that includes earning ability.

Okay. But when the second income overshadows the male's, problems can occur. The truth of the matter is, as we have stated, most men do make more money than their spouses or partners and are glad of it. That's part of The Code. And, because of the historical roles we all bring into our relationships, it generally feels right to both husband and wife. However, as women grow stronger in the work force and begin to get paid fairly, this earning trend is changing, albeit slowly. It creates new questions, as the following letter indicates:

Dear Dr. Towery:

I am in my mid-forties and make a decent income as a CPA. My problem is that my wife makes bigger bucks as a corporate attorney and regards her income as totally supplementary. That's a nice way of saying she indulges herself frequently with expensive jewelry, and boards two horses at an outlandishly expensive barn.

What really gets to me is that I have to pay all of the normal bills, such as the mortgage, insurance, car payments — every-

thing. I also have to pay alimony from a previous marriage. I barely get by and my wife pretends we don't have a care in the world. She throws a fit when I ask her to pick up a utility bill. But I'm getting more and more impatient with this and am not going to take it much longer. You write for men. What should I do?

For both men and women, I think it's important to remember that it's difficult to let go of the deep-seated conviction that men should be the primary provider — even if he makes less money. And in so doing, the man should be stronger, smarter — in a word, more masterful. It's important for us not to be too hard on ourselves. Both sexes need to understand that this is a difficult transition and one that will take much communication and understanding to work through.

In situations such as the one above, it doesn't make sense for the woman's money to be viewed as supplemental while the man's money covers all of the joint bills. It's not fair. It's one of the double standards that work against men today. How would a woman feel in a reverse situation?

And neither should the woman be in the position of financing all of the man's dreams. There needs to be a healthy compromise. Talk about it. Fight about it if you need to. But don't sweep it under the carpet. It will mess you up down the line.

Building together

One nice thing about strong relationships is the building of common dreams. Dreams are much nicer if you share them. When both parties are capable of achieving independent success, it becomes more critical to weave dreams together. Find something you both want. A cottage in the country, a kite-making business — it doesn't matter what it is — but work toward that goal *together*. Otherwise, you build separate empires. And in a partnership, nobody wins at that game.

I'm not sure who originally said this, but I know one man that did: the English comedian Benny Hill. He used to play a deranged schoolteacher who would write on the blackboard, "When you ASSUME, you make an ASS out of U and ME." And it cuts both ways. Don't assume that your male partner has his ego crushed when you bring home that bigger paycheck. Give him some credit; maybe he's got his priorities straight and could care less. And don't assume that your female partner resents that you make less than she does. Dollar signs equaling lovability probably crosses your mind far more than it does hers. Talk it out and see.

The castration dilemma

To address another powerful stereotype, women who make more money, gain more status, or just win a tennis match, claim they are accused of castrating their male. A female benefits analyst with a Fortune 500 company offers the following example. She makes roughly twice the salary as her scholarly husband who writes political tracts and teaches part time at a local state college:

John and I have come to terms with our salary differential. But I think we had something very important in our favor. Namely, success isn't that much of an issue for me. . . . My mother is a physician, my father a successful banker. I was encouraged to do as well as my two brothers in school. I was praised for being independent. And my husband comes from a similar background. His mother is a research assistant at a university. His father is a journalist. Both of them make pretty much the same amount of money. So, we didn't come into this marriage thinking of him as big provider, me little provider. I think that helps a lot. I think it's expectations that kill couples.

The backlash many women report when they become successful is undoubtedly a result of breaking the *status quo,* or the unwritten social contracts between men and women. Acknowledging the power of these contracts is the first and most important step to understanding them and dealing with them. What we cannot do is keep one foot in the "old way of doing things" and give lip service to the new. It simply isn't working.

Dismantling the barriers

One women's rights activist I interviewed suggested that some issues have to mature before you can do something about them. This may well be the case with financial differences in relationships. Once it becomes natural to see women in all roles, even as president, then the last barriers will fall. For now, we are still in the process of change. Yes, it will take time, but that's no excuse to do nothing. We can make the transition a productive, creative one — or we can keep doing what we're doing now.

We are in the process of redefining the proper roles for men and women in this society, and it's painful. The sexes have come through a social revolution together, and we have more understanding. But each of us is still dragging our feet in some areas.

Yes, men do harbor the fear that if women can afford to leave them economically, they will. When you feel your entire worth as a man depends on money, it's threatening to see her purse getting bigger than your wallet.

"But think of the value of knowing that when women do embark on a career, become successful, and then choose to continue in the relationship, what that means," my political activist friend says. It means the women are making a choice in partners based on caring for the individual man — not his earning power. Then the man knows it is he she values, not only that he can earn more money than she. And that can bring about a new level of marital harmony.

CHAPTER SEVEN

WOMEN AS TROPHIES

Question for women: Do you think more men are starting to view
achievement-oriented women as trophies?

During one of my seminars, a female management consultant quipped: "I think the new attraction for men is to the successful woman. She's become the new glamorous woman."

She argued that women in power are *very* glamorous these
days. However, it is a rare man, she suggests, who has the ability
to take one of these women home. This is true both in the sense
of being able to spark the woman's attention, and his ability to
handle her achievement.

The heart of the matter: Trophy or Trouble

In society today there is a duality of messages, a new double
standard for women: "Go ahead and be successful, but not too
successful."

As the consultant suggests, many men are attracted to successful women. It's not so surprising — even for men governed
by The Code. Ever since The Code fell into place eons ago, men
fought for the largest caves, the best tools, and the best women.

During workshops, I have found many men are adamant on
this subject, indicating that they are attracted to independent,
career-oriented women. Many translate it into: "Of course, I want
the best!"

One minister said the toughest period of his eleven-year
marriage was when his wife stayed at home with the children, and

he felt he was not only the sole supporter but *her* sole source of entertainment. And many men also take sincere pride in the achievements of their spouses. As a health-care administrator in his late thirties explains, "Men are trophy-oriented. So there is definitely an element of pride in introducing your pretty wife, the LAWYER, or ADVERTISING MOGUL, or whatever." However, he went on to confess that he would "probably not like his wife to be more successful than he."

The positives are that the woman is no longer totally dependent. She is a partner in every sense of the word. As the health-care executive notes, these women are usually more sophisticated and, in general, are better skilled communicators.

In personal relationships, the notion of the successful, completely independent woman also shifts the balance of power. This woman doesn't need the status attached to being Mrs. CEO or Mrs. Brain Surgeon. Dr. Harriet B. Braiker, writing for *Working Woman,* points out that high-achieving women present a different type of challenge for their male partners: "If a woman doesn't *need* to stay with you in order to get your status or money, then you have to work at keeping her with affection, with sexuality — in other words with yourself."[20]

But a high-powered female "trophy" can threaten a man to his psychological core. She not only can provide her own meal ticket and her own status, but she is often surrounded by other highly successful, interesting males. Taking business trips presents a threat, causing concern that she will meet more attractive and exciting potential partners as her role/responsibilities in a job expand.

Will she leave me?

The question then becomes: Will she leave me? And this is not always unwarranted concern on the part of men. I have both interviewed and worked with many women who admit that they began losing interest in their husbands, at least temporarily, as they started business jetting around the country. Staying in classy hotels, going to fancy restaurants with male business colleagues (who seem totally sophisticated and charming) can make their husband, "the accountant," look boring by comparison.

In this vein, I was struck by the candor of Ken Olin, the star of the hit series *thirtysomething*. In an interview for *TV Guide*, he discussed the effect of working with his real-life wife, Patricia Wettig, on the set of the show.[21] Although married to different people in the series, in real life the couple share a fast-paced work schedule and full family life complete with children. Speaking on his wife's success, Olin admits that he fears being left for someone who is more interesting or intelligent.

If she becomes more successful, Olin confesses, it would be very difficult for him: "I think it would be very complicated for me. I think it has to do with the competitive need that men have, just sort of this deep-seated competition among men, about your measure of success. And so within the home, if you are coming in second, I think it's very difficult. Maybe she will meet some bigger, better guys. . . ."[22]

It would be nice to attribute his fear to the part of The Code that tells a man he has to be the best — and dismiss his fear as unwarranted. But the truth is not so simple. Couples can outgrow each other, and it is no longer simply a case of men attaching to younger, more fascinating, or more intelligent women. Women are often drawn to men whom they view as a "success object." So, in reality, some women leave a man if he scores poorly in one category, be it his job, sexual techniques, or any of the other scales where men are judged.

Janice is a case in point. Married for seventeen years to her college sweetheart, she returned to school to earn an MBA. Three years out of school, she landed the job of her dreams with a pharmaceutical firm. The job meant extensive traveling to New York and Chicago and several West Coast cities. It also meant dining and partying with her peers and physicians in five-star restaurants. Her husband, Ed, who had stayed in the same stable, but not-so-exciting manufacturing job, started looking dull by comparison. As she puts it:

I grew up in a small Southern city. In fact, it was a big deal that I went away to college, because most of my girlfriends married and settled down right after high school — if not before. My husband came from the same type background, and frankly, all I thought about was my future as a wife and mother. As our daughter grew up and became independent, I became restless. My husband didn't.

When I went back to school, I knew it was creating tension. Tension from the fact that I was reaching for change. Then, when I went to work with an exciting company, I started meeting men who shared my enthusiasm for new ideas, new experiences — and I don't necessarily mean sexually. But it was an excitement for the new that was missing in Ed and it was something I couldn't make happen in him. I divorced him about a year into the job. Sure, I guess you could say it's the job that did it. He wasn't somebody I could come home to anymore. Dissolving our marriage was very painful. Painful but necessary.

Janice's story brings up an interesting point. When tremendous change is occurring, it is probably more difficult for the men in marriages to adapt, than for men who choose to be with highly successful women from day one. The latter group knows what they are bargaining for, and hopefully, they know they want it.

But it is wrong to say that men in long-term marriages where the woman chooses to challenge herself are always uncomfortable or intimidated. One judge I interviewed, for example, recalls the first decade of his marriage to a traditional homemaker:

As a young trial lawyer, the last thing I thought I wanted, quite frankly, was a challenge when I came home. My wife and I have three sons and she's a wonderful mother. But, and this is a big "but," I started to notice that she was talking to me like a child. She even started using the same gibberish-type expressions women do with young children. I began visualizing myself another ten years into the marriage and the picture looked bleak. I was tired of gibberish!

Fortunately, my wife decided to go back and get her degree. I was relieved at the time because, in a selfish sense, it gave me more time to myself. In fact, it gave me more time to have an affair — something that was looking more and more appealing to me. But something I would never have predicted began to happen. My wife started talking about interesting subjects, and I started valuing her opinions. Now, she is successful in politics and I'm delighted. I'm proud of her. It was the best thing she could have done for herself, and for our marriage.

Resolving achievement conflicts

Generally speaking, men do not want to be outdone. That's basic to The Code. However, I think it has far less to do with ego gratification than women usually assume. It has everything to do with their fear of rejection. If there is one thing many women fail to understand, it is how deeply ingrained the fear of rejection is in the male. If you begin with an understanding of this fear, then resolving achievement conflicts becomes easier. Not simple, but easier.

One of the most destructive things that a woman can do is to hide her intelligence or achievements from a man. I've heard of women who hide their Phi Beta Kappa keys in an effort not to intimidate men. What eventually happens, though, is that her intelligence manifests itself, and the man does indeed feel intimidated. Perhaps the man shouldn't be with her in the first place. Perhaps he's too chauvinistic to want a woman by his side who is that capable. The point is, however, that deception only works for so long.

Similarly, I've heard of women who have turned down promotions because they are fearful that their husbands will leave them. Unfortunately, as the resentment quietly builds, it is usually the woman who feels so hemmed in and stifled that she wants to leave. That original fear backfires.

Men want to be proud of their partners. Sometimes this is for the pure satisfaction of seeing their partner become all they can, sometimes for the egotistical purpose of showing them off as a possession.

When the woman's career takes on a more successful glow than her male partner's, it can become a source of embarrassment or anger for him. It shouldn't, but we have to be realistic and say it sometimes does. The only way to work through this is to address it. As painful as this might be, ignoring it will make it worse.

On a positive note, more men are learning to live with — and love — high-achieving women. But that's not true of all men. A woman needs to decide if she should play a game of pretend, or risk finding out what kind of man she is really dealing with.

Hopefully, she is with a man who appreciates her skills and abilities. Either way, she is better off living with the truth.

CHAPTER EIGHT

WHY CHILDREN CHANGE THE PICTURE

Question for women: Do you feel the child-rearing responsibili-
ties fall in your domain and that you must
act as interpreter between your children
and their father?

How can a working mother and father raise children? It is
difficult for couples to answer, especially if the woman's work
calls for her to travel or work late hours. This situation is the
turning point for many men. It's not a question so much of
"Where is my wife headed in her career?" as "What is she leaving
behind?" If what they are leaving behind is a child or children,
then men's concern takes on a new dimension.

While it would be easy to say that the man should stay home
with the children in this situation — this is a new era after all —
it simply is not realistic. It's unrealistic because it undermines the
male's career — an option most women in two-career families
find equally unacceptable.

The movie, *Kramer vs. Kramer,* for example, poignantly
illustrates what happens to a father who becomes the primary
caretaker of the couple's young son. Caught up in the fast-paced
world of Madison Avenue advertising, the father rudely discovers
how unsympathetic the business world is to parental demands: he
is fired.

Men are as negatively impacted by stereotypes as women.
What we have witnessed in the few states with parental leave
statutes, is that most men are reluctant to stay at home with the
children. They are reluctant for the same reasons that women are;

namely, that they think they will be perceived as less serious about their careers.

Many men also think it adversely affects their ability to be promoted. I think these men's perceptions are correct. There are only six states (Connecticut, Maine, Minnesota, Oregon, Rhode Island, and Wisconsin) that have passed laws requiring employers to give both mothers and fathers time off when they have a new baby or a seriously ill child.

But are men taking advantage of the new legislation? Studies show that men who stay at home for a week or more are still in the minority. For example, a 1986 study of 384 companies revealed that while more than one-third of the businesses offered unpaid paternity leave, only a handful of men took it.[23]

Why is this? Remember when you were a teenager and everything you ever did was because of "peer pressure." There's probably a lot of that going on here. When men look around, they don't see the top executives — or anyone else for that matter — asking for time off for parenting. And there is still the lingering suspicion that this culture doesn't sanction it.

Things are changing, however. Studies of 6,600 Du Pont workers showed that men's interest in flexible work schedules has doubled in the past few years.[24] Only 18 percent said they wanted the option of part-time work to allow them to stay at home with their children in 1985. By 1988, 33 percent claimed they did.

And, according to a Boston University study on balancing job and home life, 74 percent of the fathers said they should share child-care chores equally with the mother. Not surprisingly, only 13 percent do share the chores equally with mom. In fact, mothers average almost 44 hours per week on home/child-care activities, while fathers averaged close to 27 percent.[25]

A general uneasiness

There is still a general uneasiness for men when it comes to changing diapers or feeding and bathing a small child. Most fathers today have no role model for such activities. Robert, a thirty-five-year-old father who owns a small graphics business told me:

> *When I come home, I help my wife take care of the two boys. She wants to stay at home and be with them, but she also works at night at her own design business. I don't think if the roles were reversed that I could stay with them all day. It's hard work, and I honestly don't see how she does it. I guess I'm lucky because she wants to.*
>
> *Even so, there are times when my helping out feels uncomfortable. When my Mom comes over and sees me washing dishes and changing diapers, she gives me a disapproving look — as if I married the wrong girl. I hate it, and it makes me feel uncomfortable. I know I should pitch in, but I don't always think I do such a great job with the boys. Can I help it if it still feels "unmanly"?*

Reconciling the work ethic and parenting

Americans have never reconciled the work ethic with the demands of parenting. The business world acknowledged the validity of women in the work place. Now it needs to accept the validity of parental concerns and not assume that they are in direct conflict with productivity.

But the reverse is often true. A recent study shows that married women are the most satisfied in their jobs. Contrary to popular myth, single women who can focus completely on their careers report the greatest dissatisfaction with their jobs. These results suggest that a supportive family life can enhance, rather than compete with a woman's job performance.[26]

If corporate America has learned anything, it is that healthy, happier employees are the most productive. Yet from personal experience with some pretty high-powered companies, I can testify that a man who takes a year off from his job to be a housefather can kiss his career with the company goodbye.

Married men report the greatest satisfaction with their lives of any group within our society. To take that one step further, husbands with successful wives are happier with their marriages, according to Philip Blumstein and Pepper Schwartz in their book, *American Couples: Money, Work and Sex.*[27]

On the bright side, there are three factors that may push American businesses to reconcile the demands of parenting with the demands of working: (1) the entrance of more and more women into management roles; (2) an increasing number of fathers who watch their daughters trying to balance career and family issues; and (3) companies becoming more product- or results-oriented, rather than rule-oriented.

In this last category, many smaller companies are becoming more flexible with work schedules in order to capture a talented pool of employees. These same workers are exiting the large corporations because of the inflexible, eight-to-five mentality of management.

The parent of last resort

Syndicated columnist Ellen Goodman once remarked that, "fathers are the parent of last resort." She may be right, but it certainly isn't funny. Many of today's fathers want very much to be more than silent observers in the family circle. However, the current generation of fathers were brought up to be successful in the work arena, not on the home front. At the basic level, most fathers spend long hours at work because they feel that is where they can be most productive — and do the family the most good by making money.

Coping with daycare

As parents drop off their kids in daycare on the way to work, they are faced with a tough question: How do you nurture children in the midst of two careers that demand time and energy?

How do you balance the financial needs of your children with the emotional needs? And without a doubt, the longer *HER* hours, the more *SHE* travels, the more the father generally worries.

For parents who leave their children from nine to five, there are ways to help cope. Talking it over with the child is extremely helpful if he or she is old enough to understand. Do not skip this option. Children are often much smarter than we give them credit for and can pick up on things that need to be explained. Children enjoy being considered "part of the team" and generally respond positively when they understand their role and obligations.

Both parents can make home life a priority. By this I mean both the mother and father can decide how much travel is really necessary for their careers and cut back if possible. Also, we need to question our real motives for hanging around late at the office. As one editor who always stayed until 9:00 every night discovered, we reach a point of diminishing return.

What I eventually discovered is that I wasn't doing much from 8:00 to 5:00, because I was counting on working late anyway. I realized that I was playing a game with myself, and I would be helping myself and my family if I quit earlier each day. Also, unconsciously I felt that I was making points by being the martyr who always worked late. In truth, no one respected me for it.

It is also beneficial to draw the line clearly between home and work. Too many men and women bring work home, and then feel "invaded" when their family asks them to participate in normal events, such as a school football game. The family has a right to expect you to "be there for them," and that doesn't mean sequestered in the study or home office.

Making simple events special is also easy with children. One publisher, for example, received a children's book from his secretary. The secretary said it was on sale and she thought his small daughters would enjoy it since it was a story about a rabbit. As he later reflected:

It was a little gift, but it taught me a valuable lesson. I really bonded with my daughters the evening I brought it home and read it to them. My youngest fell asleep with the book in her arms.

You don't have to buy children a $100 stuffed toy for them to feel special or to feel noticed. Children, more so than adults, appreciate the moment. Today is very important to them. They don't necessarily understand that you will make the time up to them tomorrow or next week. What they do understand is your being with them today.

Finally, don't kid yourself. Being a working parent is extremely stressful. Don't fall into the myth of Superdad or Supermom. There's no such animal. Instead, find ways to cope with the stress, be it exercise, a hobby, reading, whatever.

Be honest about your limitations, too. And realize that you are shortchanging others when you try to keep it all inside you. To contend that you are sacrificing yourself for your family by working ridiculous hours is a lie, and you should acknowledge it.

Establishing fair guidelines

In realistic terms, there are no one-step solutions. Rearing children together requires compromise and tradeoffs.

A compromise might mean that one of the parents puts his or her career on hold for a while. Shirley, a thirty-year-old active mother of three, found a workable solution:

Ever since I earned my law degree, I have considered myself a professional woman. Our first child wasn't planned, and I ended up working long hours and leaving Stacey in daycare. Stacey is a wonderful, quiet girl who seemed to intuitively understand the situation. However, the long hours away diminished our relationship. I grew more and more depressed, but I couldn't even figure out what was making me feel so badly.

After my second child, I realized that I wanted to stay at home with him for at least the first year. It was a wonderful

*experience. I never dreamed I would feel so rewarded by chil-
dren. In fact, during that period, my biggest battle was putting up
with feminists who thought I had "copped out." I hated them and
hated me for worrying about the issue.*

*Now Stephen (my husband) and I have three children. I plan
to stay at home for another couple of years. Stephen didn't make
the decision for me — for us. I made it myself. Sometimes I do
worry about how much damage I've done my professional career
by dropping out. I don't kid myself that it will be easy reentering
the job market. But this is simply a choice I had to make, and I
wouldn't have it any other way.*

Shirley had the courage to follow her heart. She realized she
made a tradeoff with her career. Perhaps more importantly, she
took full responsibility for the decision. Rather than follow the
lead of some by blaming the "good ole boy" network for her
career slipping, Shirley acknowledged that this is what she chose
to do, fully aware of the consequences.

Ted Koppel represents another more well-known example
of compromise. He took several years off from his broadcast
career to stay with his children while his wife finished her law
degree. I don't hear anyone arguing that the host of ABC's
Nightline "damaged his career," but he may be an exception. His
star-quality network position probably gave him protection not
enjoyed by men with more mundane positions.

For many working couples, there may not be a choice. It is
estimated that 52 percent of the women with children age three
and under are in the work force, and that approximately 85 percent of these women don't have an economic option. They can't
afford to stay at home with their children. '

If you are a parent who must leave your children, there are
ways to find help. Review your schedule carefully to make sure
you are maximizing your time. Good time management skills
belong in everyone's life.

Work out a schedule with your partner, one that you both
can agree on. Start with the idea that the schedule should be fair

to all concerned. And don't be afraid to experiment.

Finally, don't neglect to talk to other parents in the neighborhood or at school about how they handle the pressures. You may well be surprised at the options other people can uncover for you.

CHAPTER NINE

THE GLASS CEILING IN RELATIONSHIPS

Question for women: Does your career present a catch-22 in your relationship? Do you feel that your partner wants you to achieve success, but not to the point where his male ego is threatened?

The ultimate "accessory" for the successful man, as the saying goes, is a beautiful woman — not necessarily an intelligent woman, or a high achiever. Who, for instance, attracted no less than two Kennedys (John and Bobby), one of the most respected playwrights of this century (Arthur Miller), and one of the greatest baseball players to ever put on cleats (Joe DiMaggio)? Marilyn Monroe. Mental giant? Questionable — although she was more intelligent than generally assumed. Corporate wizard? Absolutely not. But she was sheer, seductive beauty in its rawest essence.

Ads, in this "enlightened age," are stuffed with classically beautiful female models, most extremely young. These sexy sirens embrace us from the pages of virtually every magazine, serving as part and parcel of the POWERFUL man's realm — along with a few other standards, such as 18-karat-gold Rolex watches, bottles of Dom Perignon, oriental rugs, polo ponies, and a Mercedes-Benz.

The same is true in other media. In television commercials, long, leggy women are packaged with the more expensive cars. There's never been a doubt in my mind that the more expensive a perfume, the more beautiful the women who wear it, if you believe the advertisers. The men who make the most money can, like today's new woman, have it all. The advertisers even suggest that these men have perfect children, who play quiet games on the oriental rugs alongside their trendy Chinese Shar-Pei puppies or shaded-silver Persian cats. No muss, no fuss, no accidents.

Talk about rewards for being true to The Code! Kill the biggest bear, bring home the most money, and you win the jackpot.

The glass ceiling

But what about women who are successful in their own right? There seems to be a threatening message that she can be successful, but not *too* successful. In a sense, there is a glass ceiling in personal relationships for women, just as in the corporate world. There's a double-edged message that can be summed up as, "Be good, but not too good, honey."

After all, in America's primetime soaps, do nice women supersede the male superior? No. In *Dynasty*, Alexis Carrington Colby could run a comparable empire to Blake Carrington, but is she a good woman? She's evil incarnate. A bitch's bitch. The softer, lovable, desirable Krystle (secretary-cum-heiress) would never think of eclipsing husband Blake's success. In what are considered *avant-garde* prime time television shows, such as *L.A. Law* or *thirtysomething*, does a woman who is more powerful, more successful than the man in her life, have a healthy personal relationship? I don't think so.

At one point in the *L.A. Law* series, Deputy District Attorney Grace van Owen might be toe-to-toe professionally with her lover, private practice lawyer Michael Kuzak, but she did not overshadow him. Actually, her stability was questionable at times. During the first season, she had a terrible time getting over being shot by the friend of a criminal defendant, and she became addicted to drugs and alcohol in the process. Of course, she has since made a miraculous recovery.

Similarly, there is one married couple on the legal staff, Ann Kelsey and Stuart Markowitz (played by real-life husband and wife team, Michael Tucker and Jill Eikenberry). But is Ann a true competitor? No. Subtly, you are lead to believe that Stuart is a tax genius.

Although she wins a lawsuit from time to time, it is never implied that Ann is a genius in one area of the law. As if to make certain that the issue of competition is forever put to rest, he is a multimillionaire in his own right, having inherited a large fortune. He is capable of buying her anything.

The only happy marriage portrayed on *thirtysomething* was one in which wife/mother, Hope Steadman, was a homemaker. No career conflicts here. But a few of the right points are in place: she is sensitive, articulate. She is also college educated, sophisticated, and worries about being the right type of mother.

Later in the series when she became more concerned about her career, the "perfect marriage" foundered. Evidently, it became too much for her to follow Michael around. The series almost closed with Hope and Michael separating, except in the very last episode they (sanely) decided their marriage was more important than career points.

What's with the media

It's tempting to say that something is wrong with the media; more specifically, that something is wrong with the writers of these series. But these people are not dumb brutes. Nor are they all chauvinist pigs. *Dynasty*, for example, was coauthored by a husband and wife team, Esther and Richard Shapiro. Emmy-winning *L.A. Law* was coauthored by Steven Bochco and Terry Louise Fisher. What these writers were doing was appealing to our deepest fantasies — particularly those of women, since female viewers roughly outnumber male viewers two-to-one for many nighttime soaps.

Surveys conducted by New York City-based Arbitron Ratings Company demonstrate that women, age eighteen and over, are the primary audience of these programs.[28] For example, the random-sample sweep conducted during February 3 to March 1,

1988 (which covers the continental United States), showed that *Dynasty* netted approximately 13 percent of the total potential female audience (age eighteen and over), but only 7 percent of the total number of men during an average week.

Arbitron's survey sweep from April 27 through May 24, 1988, showed the estimated weekly audience of major nighttime soaps to be primarily women:

	Females (age 18 and over)	Males (age 18 and over)
Dallas	15,746,000	8,556,000
L.A. Law	12,613,000	9,893,000
thirtysomething	8,178,000	4,878,000

These numbers are telling us something. The more affluent the setting, such as oil barons in Dallas, or rich lawyers in Los Angeles, the more audience appeal. In *thirtysomething*, which netted the fewest viewers, the men and women were still struggling financially. *Dallas*, which led the pack, portrayed women as successful only in terms of the males they attracted.

These stereotypes are damaging. There isn't a single female character in *Dallas* who earned an advanced degree. These are strictly women who look like they live in beauty salons and designer shops, and somehow that gives them the right to spend a male oil baron's money.

Even Miss Ellie wasn't immune. She *inherited* her beloved ranch, South Fork, from Daddy. Don't get me wrong, she was a nice woman. But where would Miss Ellie be if she had grown up under ordinary circumstances?

What we have to ask ourselves is what type of message does this script relay to an eighteen-year-old girl — or boy? It tells the young lady that, by and large, the single most important quality is beauty. It tells the teenage boy that he damn well better make money, and not just decent money, but lots of money.

Sound like The Code? Men don't win because they are team players. They win because they're willing to stand alone and win at all costs.

The new fantasy

To move away from soaps, the movie *Arthur* is perhaps a better example of how the new fantasy plays out. The lovable, if not weak, Arthur is a billionaire. He is slated to marry a cold but oh-so-rich young woman from his family's social setting. But, as fantasy would have it, he falls in love with a waitress. Not just any waitress, but one who is zany, humorous, and good hearted.

What is interesting here, is that she is studying to be an actress at night. (In the old movies she would have been a pretty waitress, period.) That she has some aspiration — other than marrying money — is important for today's movie-going market. It's probably why the plot worked for so many moviegoers.

The same is true for *Flashdance*. Does Nick fall in love with just *any* welder in his steel company? Not by a long shot. Number one, it doesn't hurt that she is beautiful and sexy. But it also helps that she has a personal dream — a dream to be a great ballerina.

Never mind that she had to be eighteen years old to be working as a welder, and most ballerinas are nearing the peak of their careers by the time they hit their early twenties — after a decade or more of rigorous training. Bold knight in a black Porsche to the rescue. Someone to finance her dream, as Dr. Warren Farrell points out in his book, *Why Men Are the Way They Are*.[29]

What can be observed in these new fantasies are variations of the old ones. Look at the blockbuster, *Pretty Woman*. The heroine is a beautiful young woman who has a bit of financial difficulty and turns to prostitution. You are immediately cued that she's basically a wonderful girl who's really not cut out for life on the streets. She's charming, funny, and gutsy. She has a good heart. She's also the typical damsel in distress waiting for a handsome, brilliant, and very rich man to save her. The perfect American love story.

All these fantasies play into The Code. The strong, silent hero, who happens to have infinite financial resources, can rescue the beautiful woman. He thereby wins her heart and earns a blissful future. It could be Hollywood in the 1940s. However, an important transition has occurred. The knights don't rescue just any damsel — not like in the old movies. She must be a feisty damsel with talent. Perhaps most importantly, she must have a talent that will not eclipse his own.

The fantasy plays in many different ways. In *Broadcast News,* does the intelligent Aaron fall for a simple girl? Not on your life. He is head over heels in love with Jane, a sassy, brilliant producer. For her part, can she reciprocate Aaron's love? No. She is completely enthralled by Tom Grunick, an empty, albeit good-looking, anchor man. Tom has two important qualities that play into the Great American fantasy: he makes a great deal of money and Jane cannot eclipse him because top anchor men are the stars of network news, not the producers.

Does any boy get girl in *Broadcast News*? You are led to believe that Aaron does find someone to settle down with and have his children — but not Jane, the great love of his life. In the end we find Jane dating someone, and Tom is set to marry a beautiful but equally empty young woman.

At least this script asks us to question our fantasies. What I think is most touching about this movie are Aaron's lines to Jane when they are talking about the difficulty of male-female relationships. In his words: "Wouldn't this be a great world if insecurity and desperation made us more attractive? If needy were a turn on?" How true. Men like Aaron would get the girl.

A not-so-delicate balance

For better or worse, what is popular in the media is popular for one reason: it holds a mirror to our society. What we are seeing is a new, subtler form of discrimination in the success arena. In personal relationships, it's okay for the woman to have dreams of success. She can even be successful, like Jane in *Broadcast News*. Yet, the man must still be the more powerful partner. Echoes of The Code.

The truth is we have not let go of the notion that men should be taller, richer, older, smarter, stronger, and more worldly than women. If one of these cues is reversed, society raises its collective brows. That is not the fault of men. It's not the fault of women. That is simple fact.

A successful female publicist told me her story:

When I was thirty-five, I married a man ten years my junior. He was an aspiring musician who made pizza during the day. I will never forget the look on my best friend's face when I announced the engagement. It was one of shock, then pity. In fact, later that same evening she pulled me aside to say, "I could never do what you are doing. I admire you. Money's too important to me." Of course she did not admire me. She pitied me for marrying "beneath myself," and missing my opportunity to capture a "status provider." In the course of the next year, our friendship crumbled. She seemed to make a point of telling me the type of couples she and her husband were entertaining. They were physicians and their wives; accountants and psychologists; lawyers and every "profession" under the sun. One day, I found myself fantasizing that my husband single-handedly built a huge pizza parlor empire and we were worth millions. That would show her. Then, I realized I was letting my values become the same as hers. She hurt me deeply.

What this woman discovered is that it isn't always what men think — or one particular man thinks — about a woman's success. It is a societal issue. If the woman goes into the market and brings home the bacon (i.e., a bigger paycheck than her husband), she faces a long list of social taboos that *she* must have the courage to confront. Few women aspire to take care of a man financially, and when one does, it presents a serious threat to most people's *status quo*.

A comfortable place

What men and women are trying to achieve is a comfort

zone in which they can express individual values. We haven't reached that point, and it may take a few generations to realize that we don't have to accept extreme positions. Just because one woman wants to be highly successful and support herself — and possibly her husband — doesn't mean that she is defining that lifestyle for all women.

One of the most serious stumbling blocks in the women's movement has little to do with chauvinism. It has more to do with the fear of many women that they are going to be required to forfeit something, and there will be nothing to take its place. Ann Marie, a licensed social worker, identifies the quandary many women find themselves in:

I married for security. Not big money, but let's just say I knew my husband was going to pay the mortgage. I also consider myself a feminist. I would be furious, for example, if the state thought it could pay me less because I am a female social worker.

However, I hesitate to stand up as a libber. I don't like this idea that it's either one way or the other. I love my husband. I love his willingness to care for me and the children. I like those traditional male and female roles. I guess I want the best of both worlds, and I'm afraid too many feminists are going to destroy the good with the bad.

The same is true for many men. There seems to be a lingering fear that to give in on one issue, means to give in on all. When men retrace their steps, they realize that compromise is valid and doesn't mean they have given the shop away. Otherwise, reaching an agreement is much more difficult than it needs to be. As one male reader puts it:

Dear Dr. Towery:

I've reached a point with my wife where I can't win. I've worked hard since I was 16 years old. I never thought about doing anything but work, and making a good living. Now my wife says I don't do enough around the house. What is so wrong with me

*making a living, and her taking responsibility for the home? I
don't expect her to work. If she wants to work, that's fine, too. But
now it's the woman's way or no way.*

Finding a way out isn't easy, but a great place to start is to
realize that a man can give in on one issue without defining
himself as a wimp. Similarly, a woman can want a traditional
family and not necessarily be anti-women's movement.

For positive change to occur, it's important to avoid small,
one-issue battles. For example, the social worker who enjoys
having her husband pick up the mortgage isn't killing the women's
movement any more than the man who wants his wife to take care
of the home.

Many of both sexes want to take the best of the traditional
and merge it with the best of the new roles. There's nothing
unusual about that. While not always possible, taking a right-
wrong, black-white stance on traditional roles versus the new
roles is dangerous. It's dangerous because it leaves everyone
afraid of change.

CHAPTER TEN

LOVERS AS RIVALS — MAKING IT WORK

Question for women: How can I be my best without intimidating a man?

In terms of male-female issues, today's society is eons different from just twenty years ago. Men and women are now free to compete intellectually and physically (in some sports). We men often have difficulty handling it, but the male's so-called fragile ego isn't the only component coming into play. These are *new* roles to explore.

It wasn't too many years ago, for example, that a man wouldn't *think* of playing a hard game of tennis with a woman. Role expectations would have dictated two things: (1) that it was unmanly to physically challenge a woman; and (2) it was unthinkable that the match would be a true challenge, i.e., that he could be beaten by a woman. The sheer awkwardness of the challenge was, for years, enough to keep men playing with other men.

Marines aren't found in dollhouses

Obviously, many of our old attitudes hark back to caveman days when men challenged tigers and bears, not womenfolk. Women gathered nuts and berries, took care of the children, and, in general, kept the hearth fires burning. In our role playing, we haven't advanced that far. We still encourage little boys to be more physical. Let's face it, Marines aren't recruited from dollhouses. We still train men to die for causes. Not women.

77

Women were — and some still are — trained to compete on one turf: for men. A woman, in many instances, gains status in direct proportion to the male to whom she attaches.

Architect or victim?

That's one way of saying that this is a difficult issue. But we live in an era that calls for the courage to change, as Wendy Reid Crisp, a former editor at *Savvy*, poignantly points out in her "Editor's Note" for the October, 1985 issue of the magazine.[30] Quoting from Merikay McLeod's book, *Betrayal*, she writes, "Change is inevitable. We will always exist in the midst of it. It is our choice whether we will be its victim or its architect."

McLeod's book recounts her equal pay class action against Pacific Press, a Seventh Day Adventist publishing house in California. Her battle was an admirable one, especially in the context of the author's upbringing. She was a mere twenty-five years old at the time, married and a devout Seventh Day Adventist on her first job. But when her husband lost his job, she could not afford to pay the rent.

The conclusions McLeod draws from her struggle, though, are incomplete, according to Crisp, who is now publisher of New York City-based New Chapter Press. "One does not choose to become either a victim or an architect of change; rather, truly effective people are required to assume both roles." And McLeod was certainly both. In the midst of her struggle, she lost her friends, her marriage, and her job — she was fired as a result of her lawsuit. It took great courage to demand change.

What both sexes are learning is that we are both victims and architects in a new social order — an order that asks us to rethink roles that were completely acceptable a short two decades ago.

Letting go

Many of the role expectations are difficult to let go of, and one that is particularly stubborn is that women are not supposed to outdo men. Women are supposed to be quiet little stars in men's constellations — not rocket scientists who blow men out of the universe. And many women today are still afraid that autonomous success will render them unlovable and alone.

Women's view of their own success

That is why it is impossible to deal with how men view the issue without exploring how women feel about their own success. What happens in any given relationship is intrinsically tied to the notion of projection. In other words, if successful women expect to be alone, then they will be. The vibes they give off will be received, processed, and acted upon.

Carol Gilligan cites a study in her book, *In a Different Voice, Psychological Theory and Women's Development,* that pinpoints the difference between men's and women's perceptions of autonomous achievement.[31] A motivation class of eighty-eight men and fifty women was asked to interpret several pictures. Some depicted people at work and suggested achievement, such as a man sitting alone at a desk in a high-rise office building. Other pictures depicted close personal affiliation, such as a male and female trapeze artist. Men imagined danger and violence more often in the pictures that portrayed two people in close affiliation, while women perceived danger in impersonal achievement situations.

As Gilligan concludes, "Women appeared to have a problem with competitive achievement, and that problem seemed to emanate from a perceived conflict between femininity and success. . . ."[32]

By comparison, the danger men described in their stories involved intimacy and a danger of entrapment or betrayal. The perceived danger focused on being caught in "a smothering relationship or humiliated by rejection and deceit."[33]

Masculine protection

As women become competent rivals, what often comes into play is their fear of being abandoned, being condemned by their very achievements to a life alone. Women tend to feel less feminine when they can prove that they are smarter than their male partners — or when they can make more money than a man.

It's understandable. "Masculine protection" is still one of the highest privileges in this society. And it is a notion that women have preserved as tenaciously as men, if not more so. A young female sales rep gives the following example of masculine protection:

One of my best friends is married to one of the richest men in town. She's not working right now, but I can feel her clout when we're out together. It's tangible. Why, I've been at parties where bankers literally drooled on her, stumbling all over themselves to try and impress her. She even finds it humorous.

If I want to be really honest, I will tell you that women, I think, are even more impressed with her financial clout. There's something about a woman attached to a powerful man in this society that I think is more respected than a woman who makes it on her own. I can't say why that is, but I think it's an undeniable fact.

One possible explanation is that women are taught the importance of being liked. It is a primary virtue for them. And what better way to prove you are likable than being married to one of the most desirable men in the city?

"Being liked is one of the most important messages we receive as little girls," affirms Patricia B. Arnold, Ph.D., who teaches organizational behavior and theory courses at Vanderbilt University. "Men don't escape getting that message, but we get it a lot more strongly." Boys are taught (as part of The Code) the importance of winning. Everything else, they are told, is secondary.

Obstacles for men

For men, not surprisingly, a woman's success poses different challenges. It may mean he has to shift gears completely. Her success flies in the face of the time-honored role of the male as breadwinner. Taking care of his family's financial needs remains one of the safest mechanisms for a man to show his love, and this is particularly true for a man who has difficulty expressing his emotions in other ways. This is something he understands — part of The Code he learned as a child.

A major obstacle, however, as a female consultant reveals, is that men rarely make a direct issue of a woman's success. They would never say, "I want you to quit working because my self-image can't handle your success."

It would come out in much more subtle, if not destructive forms: "Our daughter Nancy is only thirteen years old — don't you think she needs to spend more time with her mother?" Or, "Our son thinks you are pushing him away. He feels shut out. He says you don't have any time for him anymore."

Adjusting to new roles

If this is the case, the only avenue open for the woman is to address the central issue. It takes time and patience to adjust to new roles. An objective third party, such as a minister or counselor, may be needed. Trying to duck the issues doesn't work.

A female lawyer, married for thirty-two years, says, "avoiding the ramifications of your success is not only stupid, it usually spells disaster. I have seen women decline promotions so they won't outshine their spouse. The resentment it breeds is deadly." A wife becomes intensely angry at her husband because of her decision, and he has no idea what is going on. If you can't talk about it, it's time to reevaluate the entire relationship, because something is seriously wrong.

A new set of values

The idea that the man is supposed to be taller, older, more successful, and smarter than the woman is deeply etched in our psyche. It is deeply ingrained in *both* sexes. And the list can be expanded to include that the man be wiser, more experienced, more courageous, and more effective in almost all areas.

It's equally unhealthy to say, "a powerful woman is the newest status symbol." We need to ignore some of the more recent media messages. For example, look at any of the popular magazines targeting professional women and see what Madison Avenue thinks success brings the professional woman. It brings her Chivas Regal with a gorgeous male. It means a man more successful than she will bring her not just an engagement ring, but a diamond that rivals the Prudential rock. You don't see many carpenters or teamsters escorting the "new woman." A tux and a Jaguar seem to be minimum requirements.

In order to deal with the new potential rivalry, it is critical for a woman to stop looking at her career victories as somehow diminishing the man in her life. Being successful is not unfeminine. Her victories represent victories not only for her, but for the couple.

Similarly, men must accept different roles within the family framework. It needs to be pointed out to men that their partners' success gives them more opportunities to romp with the kids, pursue a hobby, or perhaps take the plunge of going into business for himself — which may be what he always wanted but did not have the resources.

One career counselor I know points out that men think that their careers need to progress vertically from point A to point B to point C, with no room for digressions — or mistakes. According to The Code, autonomous success is not an option for men; it is an imperative. Women, by comparison, are not afraid to drop back, rethink their careers, and then progress to the next point slowly. As more women become full partners in a marriage, men will be able to relax from this goal-oriented posture and enjoy the financial freedom of pursuing their dreams, not dollar bills.

In this regard, one political writer recently made an interesting observation.[34] He pointed out that the yuppie (of all people) can be credited with bringing us face-to-face with what we all really fear in this society: failure. A yuppie's success is palpable. It means BMWs, designer sweat suits, and espresso.

A yuppie's failure is even more obvious. If he fails to keep up with his BMW payments, his whole identity is in crisis. If someone says, "you're a loser," it's the ultimate insult. In yuppie language, "he's dead meat."

We can all learn a valuable lesson from this. When either sex sits with a well-worn scorecard constantly trying to make lifestyle comparisons, we all fall victim to these cruel judgments. Recognizing that most of us live in a forest of superficial values is the diagnosis; laughing at them and discarding them is the treatment.

CHAPTER ELEVEN

TRAPPED: THE IMPOSSIBLE
MASCULINE MANIFESTO

Question for men: *Deep inside, are you afraid of letting others share your dreams because they might laugh at you? Because they might think you're less of a man?*

The Code can be compared to a masculine manifesto operating in society, which basically holds that a man's either tough — or he ain't. There's very little ground in between and very little forgiveness for those who fail.

Women in business have been very vocal about their own lack of effective role models over the past two decades. Instinctively, they have asked: "How can we orient ourselves for achievement when we have so few successful women in our society to emulate?"

In the wake of the women's movement, they have made important strides. To their credit, they recognize the need for strong mentors and role models if change is to occur.

What would a man do?

In comparison, men are still trapped in a masculine manifesto, a rigid formula that locks them into a one-dimensional mode. Faced with a crossroad in life, men typically sit back, with third-party objectivity, and ask: "What would a man do in this situation?"

It is rarely a matter of exploring his complex emotional side. No. You don't see many men sitting back and saying: "What do I *feel* like doing?" One twenty-eight-year-old secretary illustrates this point well in talking about her younger brother:

Monte and I are very close. We lost our father when we were both teenagers, and maybe that has something to do with his vision of manhood. He has this one idea of what it means to be a man, and no one can talk him out of it.

All he ever wanted to do was to be a concert pianist. But he never even tried. Instead, he did the safe thing and studied business.

He still plays. In fact, I wish you could see him play. He becomes a different person. His whole body becomes fluid, and he becomes one with the piano. He's going to get his MBA soon, and when we talk about it, all he can say is, "I wish Dad could be here for graduation. I think he would be proud."

I think he's right. But it's also sad. He's going to be the man somebody else thought he should be. Not the man he wanted to be. Dad wanted him to be able to appreciate music — that's why he gave us lessons. But he didn't want my brother to be a "sissy" musician. Dad used to say, "Musicians have weak characters, no morals." And my brother picked up his cue, and never let go.

Am I male enough?

Monte's story is the rule rather than the exception. Most men feel compelled to do the "male" thing, regardless of their personal dreams. It's easy to see why. In many direct and indirect ways, the male pays for attempting to break out of traditional masculine boundaries.

One quick generalization we often hear in this society, for instance, is that all hairdressers are gay. In fact, many men who enter the service sector, including waiters, interior designers, nurses, and the like, are pigeonholed as gay.

Women, by degree, have fought for and earned the right to move beyond traditional male or female role definitions. If today's woman can achieve it all — being wife, mother, business executive or construction worker — she is applauded. If she chooses to be a wife and mother, that's okay, too. Or, if she decides to stay single and pursue her career, few question her decision.

The modern male has no such freedom. The Code places him in a narrowly focused role. What happens to the majority of men who decide to stay home and be house husbands? They're ridiculed — by both men and women. People may congratulate him on his sensitive concern to his face, but behind his back, they snicker. The assumption is that he's weak — in sum, a wimp.

Stigmas are for men too

Or, what happens to the guy who stays single well into his thirties, focusing completely on his career? He's labeled. If women have fought the stigma of being an "old maid," men must contend with the stigma of being a "queer" if they never marry.

I know of a personnel manager at a Fortune 500 company who won't consider a resumé from a man over thirty who is still single. "I think most of them are gay, or want to be," he confides. "Men marry if they want to. They have a choice."

Similarly, *60 Minutes* exposed an insurance company that kicks single males over thirty out of the computer. Why? The company considers them an AIDS risk. Is that masculine privilege? No. It's discrimination.

A powerful message from the media

Rigid role models are also responsible for a number of "shutdowns" in the male's emotional makeup. They represent the dominant factor in the male's inability to communicate.

Let's take a look, for example, at who has served as the male's traditional prototype in terms of communication skills: the strong and silent type epitomized by Gary Cooper and John Wayne.

More recently, Sylvester Stallone's *Rambo* — a huge box office success — celebrates silent, brute force. Rambo personifies The Code. He is fundamentally inarticulate, a robot of destruction whose ability to communicate is limited to fighting.

Similarly, Dirty Harry is a steely-eyed man of action. I dare you to define Harry as a talented conversationalist. In fact, when Clint Eastwood stepped out of character in *Tightrope* to portray an introspective, vulnerable side, many fans complained. The message: "Get back in Code form." The fans prefer a Dirty Harry who walks it like he talks it. A silent, killing machine is idealized over a character who wrestles with his own dark side.

And how are men taught to interact with women? In the westerns, if they like a woman, they sling her over the back of their saddle and ride off into the sunset. Everybody seems happy, including the woman.

In *Why Can't Men Open Up?*, authors Steven Naifeh and Gregory White Smith look at TV westerns as prime examples of how men learn — or fail to learn — about communication and intimacy. As Smith confesses: "I was particularly devoted to the *Roy Rogers* show, at 7:00 on Sunday evenings. I think back on that show, which riveted my young attention, and I recall that the most profound emotional attachments were between Roy and his horse, Trigger, and between Pat Brady and his jeep, Nellie Belle. Needless to say, Roy and Dale never talked over their emotional problems."[35] We can even take that one step further: they never *had* emotional problems.

Old role models die hard

In any given culture, old role models die hard — as women have come to discover. Our present day Marlboro man doesn't talk. He's a cowboy! Rugged and silent to the end. The inscrutable, weather-parched face is all male. The model for Ralph Lauren's Chaps cologne doesn't do much talking either. No soft, sensitive pansy here — instead we're shown the traditional Code tough guy, complete with leather and silent appeal. Would this guy come home after a long day and share his feelings over a dinner he helped to prepare?

"Just talk to me"

And yet the single most voiced desire of today's woman concerning men is that he "just talk to me." But in fairness to men, the messages our society hands to men on the issue of communication are mixed.

Imagine: A man moves from the dinner table where his wife just asked him for the hundredth time about his feelings concerning an ethical problem in his new job. But when he sits in the family room and turns on the television to watch *Death Wish II* with her, there is a strong chance he is going to hear the wonders of Charles Bronson. She might say, "I love Bronson. There's something about him. He always gets things done."

But Bronson is a one-man vigilante hit force. He's a quiet, accomplished killing machine. He doesn't wait for justice. He *is* justice! He doesn't pussyfoot around playing verbal chess. He makes all of his points with a gun. So much for being articulate and sensitive.

Learning to laugh

A handful of role models, however, have helped change our perceptions of manhood. Woody Allen, for instance, lets us laugh *with* him when he questions his sexual prowess, or stands face to face with his own mortality.

Similarly, the type of hero Eddie Murphy portrays is more likely to make his enemies die laughing than from being shot. This humorous approach is a refreshing change from Hemingway's grueling "moment of truth" in the bullfighting ring. Hemingway not only wrote about The Code, he lived it. He also committed suicide.

But the stereotypes still haunt us. While in the movies, the powerful, inscrutable men win the wars and take the beautiful women home, the sensitive man suffers. Sadly, he often suffers alone.

In *Sophie's Choice,* does the sensitive writer, Stingo, win Sophie's love? No. She finds him touching, but she is drawn to the more powerfully charismatic, but desperately ill Nathan, who in the end brings them both death. Too often, the introspective man, the man who uses a gentle style of communication, is perceived as powerless — as powerless as the traditional female who waited patiently for the gallant knight to rescue her.

It is a gigantic problem that stops men from opening up to loved ones, not to mention other men. One of the biggest contributing factors is the male's legacy to compete. Men compete in virtually every arena of their lives: sports, business, women, possessions.

The Code fuels competition

Men learn teamwork from the sports they play growing up. The virtues of competition are impressed upon little boys, but at what a cost?

The price of "teamwork" training is steep because it means one boy constantly being compared to other boys. This inevitably carves the message in his boyish heart that other men are his competitors first, last, and always.

If you are female, the primary purpose of the games you played as a child was socialization. Whether it was jumping rope, hopscotch or dolls, you played for companionship and fun. If you are male, I assure you, there was one common denominator to your game playing: a score was always kept. Someone won; someone lost.

Rivals as friends — an untenable mix

A male never becomes really close with his rivals, for they slowly become the criteria by which he measures himself. A woman friend recently made a perceptive observation regarding this point. "When I introduce two men, they figuratively circle each other like two dogs sniffing out each other's weaknesses before they attack," she says. She couldn't be more accurate.

This situation sets the stage for very little emotional intimacy among males, something they increasingly miss as they age, but seldom are able to identify. The effect spills over into their relationships with women. Men translate a relationship into either winning or losing.

In short, you either control the emotional power base in a relationship or you lose control completely. As little boys, a vicious cycle is set in motion. Through constant conditioning, the man's world becomes surrounded by a scoreboard. And he is constantly looking over his shoulder to see how he is measuring up.

Paying your dues

It is a conditioning that has made the male athlete a hero in our society. He embodies the masculine ideal of The Code. This is the guy who plays when hurt, ignores his pain, and pursues victory at all costs.

Once he beats up other men and endures the pain stoically, he has paid his dues. And what does this entitle him to? He can now pat other men on the fanny and run his fingers through their hair. He can give them big bear hugs, hold hands, and even sit on the sidelines and cry. Ironically, it gives him the right to move beyond The Code's dictates.

But what about the businessman who hasn't paid these dues in a physical sense? Can't he show this type of emotion? I dare you to imagine two businessmen who work in the same corporation coming out of an officers' meeting, arm in arm, slapping each other's buttocks, with tears running down their faces, yelling: "We'll get 'em next time!" No corporate executive worth his wing tip shoes needs to be told it's time to hang up his three-piece suit if he pulls a stunt like that. He's finished.

Even success is a lonely place

Later in life, men wake up to find their "friends" are unable to share in their successes. One reader who recently had to deal with this situation wrote:

Dear Dr. Towery:

There's something about us men that I detest. Forget that we usually don't take the trouble to throw a life preserver to each other when we're about to go over the falls. We can't even celebrate with a friend when he has a success. Last week I made the Million-Dollar Round Table in only my second year in the insurance field. I called several friends and ended up depressed instead of happy. I felt like they were pulling away instead of rejoicing with me. Then I reflected — I do the same thing. What's wrong with us?

Retreating from a friend because of his good fortune is a typical reaction among males because of our early conditioning. The Code teaches men that failure is inexcusable. Often, another man's success causes us to feel personal failure.

A man who retires at forty, while we, at forty-two, are worrying about making our next house payment, causes us to judge ourselves pretty harshly. As long as we keep score on our lives in terms of success and failure, we will continue to judge our lives by what other men do with theirs. This is a guaranteed formula for mental and physical illness, unhappy lives, and ruined friendships.

I had a friend who owned a company along with two partners. A few years ago, the company was sold and he retired while still a young man with many millions in the bank. In retrospect,

I realize that I began avoiding him. Even when I wanted to call him for a racquetball game, I didn't. When I needed good advice that I knew he could and would give me, I didn't ask. This was not only a stupid reaction, but unfair to a good friend.

Learning to "talk"

One major way for men to combat this syndrome is to talk to their friends regularly about nothing — much the way women do. It means breaking through the barriers of The Code and not limiting conversations to business deals, which car to buy, or which mutual fund to invest in. Instead, ask about how good you feel today, what you dreamed about last night, or how hard it was to jog this morning.

In other words, talk about feelings instead of things. If we were not so goal- and success-oriented, we could ebb and flow with our friends' happinesses or misfortunes without selfishly relating them to ourselves.

Promoting healthy competition

The most profound changes, however, occur when we teach the next generation something new. That means teaching young boys a different style of competition — without constantly pitting them against each other.

While competition is an inevitable part of life, there are several steps parents can take to alleviate the pressure on sons. First and foremost is diffusing the spell of the three big sports in school: football, basketball, and baseball. These can be deemphasized by placing equal importance on different sports, even different types of achievements.

After all, when a man reaches forty, there are no football teams to be a part of, but sports such as tennis, swimming, and racquetball promote the aerobics so important to health, as well as provide a basis for companionship with other men.

Today's men might be different if they had felt equal value had been given to writing contests as to football! Or if winning a debate contest had held equal importance with playing basketball or wearing a varsity jacket.

One of the best examples of healthy competition I know of are the hunts sponsored by the Hunting Retrieving Club Inc. The purpose of these competitions is to promote excellence in retrieving dog breeds. Every dog earns points on his own, such as points when they retrieve a dummy or change course on command.

In these retriever competitions, the dogs compete only with themselves. They learn different skills, and each dog earns points as he masters each new task. That's the way sports ought to be — not a constant pitting against the other guy.

Not surprisingly, everyone is happy at these gatherings. The crowd is jubilant. They root for each other, for they are all dog lovers and want to see the retrieving breeds improve. You set out to accomplish certain things with your dog and you do them. You don't worry about the other guy. That's healthy competition.

CHAPTER TWELVE

WHEN MEN AREN'T TOUGH

Question for women: If you have sons, do you see them exhibiting archaic macho behavior such as a fascination for war games, even though you have tried to rear them as a sensitive "new man"? More importantly, are you secretly glad?

It is easy to say that an enlightened man could easily move away from The Code, simply deciding to discard behavior that negatively impacts his well-being. First of all, men don't generally make this choice objectively, but act out of instinct without realizing the source of their behavior. Secondly, men drop these learned, ingrained behaviors at great peril. It is no surprise that The Code holds a tenacious power in men's lives.

What happens, for instance, to the soft-spoken, emotive man in most office environments? He is passed over time and again for promotions, or fired — not enough fire in his belly. When a man's masculinity comes into question, he pays a dear price. Ask any gay man about job discrimination, and he can probably list many frustrating experiences. And this was true long before the AIDS crisis — which has only fueled the discrimination.

Questions to consider

Before progressing further, there are several pertinent questions for the female reader:

- Do you think it is easier to be a man in terms of not having to deal with discrimination?

- Do you think it is easier to be a man in terms of not having dual role responsibilities as nurturing parent and career demands?

- Do you assume men are never labeled, regardless of their behavior?

- Do you think men are rewarded for opening up and being the "new man"?

- As a mother, do you worry about raising an effeminate son?

- Would you cringe internally if your son started playing with his sister's Barbie Doll, even though you want your son to be sensitive and empathic?

When I present these questions in workshops, the majority of women respond "yes" to most of the questions. By comparison, most men say "no." The point is not to say there is a right or wrong response to these questions. Rather it is to show the difficulty men and women have communicating the very different and complex pressures they feel.

In the following chapters, these points and others will be addressed. The overall emphasis is not to point fingers, but to broaden awareness and understanding.

Varying faces of discrimination

That women are discriminated against in the business world is not a point of dispute. What women often fail to see, however, is the pressure men are under in the same environment. And the factors of discrimination are every bit as silly and infuriating for men as they are for women.

For example, how many top corporations are headed by short men? Few. The number is probably under five percent. Similarly, how many overweight men make it into top management? Few. How many men with high-pitched voices and effeminate gestures are allowed to progress beyond the ranks of middle management, if even that far?

Is this type of discrimination fair? Of course not. But men are caught, too, in a performance trap of trying to embody a masculine ideal that is deadly. They are given far less room to deviate than many women realize.

When a woman assumes she doesn't receive a promotion due to a sexual bias, she may be right. But I've never known a male executive to sit back and reflect: "I don't want Jane in that position. She's a woman." The guy is probably too caught up worrying about his own graying hair that may be signaling management it's time for a younger guy in his slot. Or, he may be wondering if he's on the outs because he didn't join the softball team and pitch a no-hitter for the company team.

Not making the cut

You can believe there are chauvinists. But you can also believe that men are haunted by their own list of self-doubts. The following letter illustrates what I mean:

Dear Dr. Towery:

I have worked for the same brokerage firm for five years. I have always loved where I work, but lately I have wanted to try to move away from a desk job and get into sales. I have my license and I know I have the ability. My problem is that the head of the firm says, "You aren't ready for sales. Just leave it alone for awhile."

I don't know why he won't let me try. After a couple of drinks, one of my wife's friends said, "You don't look like a salesman. You need to lose about 30 pounds and wear suits instead of sports coats. That's what an image consultant would tell you." I was furious. Why do women think it's all image?

Unfortunately, the reason this man is angry is because he realizes that there is some truth to the woman's statement. People are judged on very superficial levels at times, and corporate America is not above doing it to men and women. Looking good can be more important than being good. Like the old saying: "It's the sizzle, not the steak."

Do men have more latitude in this regard? Maybe. But not as much as women might think. Why are more men having plastic surgery these days? Plastic surgeons say it has more to do with looking younger and more fit for work than catching the eye of a new woman.

Women move with greater ease

Although they might not readily agree, women can move between feminine and masculine activities with greater ease than men. Little girls can play cowboys and Indians and no one gets upset by their tomboyish behavior. In fact, women are often complimented for being "tough," yet feminine.

A TV ad shows a female jockey maneuvering her horse through a pack of male riders to victory, and then later looking cute and sexy in her name-brand underwear. On a more serious level, journalist and TV commentator, Barbara Walters, is applauded for her piercing, "tough-minded" interviews.

That's not to say that men accept raw aggression in women. There is a line women can cross that does bring attacks from the male camp. In the movie *Broadcast News,* for example, Jane realizes she is getting too feisty for men. As she laments after her first date with her dream man, Tom: "I have passed some line, some place. I have begun to repel the people I'm trying to seduce!"

My feminist friends have also pointed out on more than one

occasion that women have a difficult time being assertive. "It's easy to be called a bitch, just for standing your ground," one said.

Labeling

But labeling cuts both ways. A man's effeminate behavior brings a sudden label of being "gay." No one applauded Truman Capote for his soft, high-pitched voice. People may have admired his writing and his wit, but his effeminate behavior prompted snickers and whispers.

The labeling can start before kindergarten. When told his little boy enjoys playing with dolls, the typical father roars: "What do you mean my little boy likes dolls!" As Dr. Georgia Witkin-Lanoil points out in her book, *The Male Stress Syndrome,* boys are expected to play war, not house.[36]

If a boy returns home from the football field and announces that he doesn't like the sport and is quitting the team, both parents may drop into a dead faint. Effeminate behavior in a little boy elicits a knee-jerk reaction from his parents and causes them to ask: "What are we doing wrong?" If their little guy isn't tough, he just isn't quite right.

There is a striking vigilance in little boys themselves to protect their own sense of masculinity — even before the age of five. They watch for signs of weakness or emotionalism. Any form of closeness might indicate a crack through which their masculinity might spill out, as Sara Bonnett Stein observes in her book, *Girls & Boys.*[37]

It is the same reason little boys love to tease and make fun of little girls. They revel in making fun of girls' fear of snakes, for example, or the fact that a little girl can't jump as high. It's typically a little boy's first efforts at protecting his masculinity, of announcing, "See, I'm stronger."

Even as adults, women are given the freedom to dress in a masculine fashion. No one thought Annie Hall was a lesbian. But men do not enjoy the same freedom.

In the 1970s, a transsexual in a southern city was contemplating a sex change operation. Under his doctor's supervision, he began dressing like a woman. The result? He was arrested for "impersonating a woman." But the prosecutor had to drop the charges when the transsexual's attorney pointed out that there was no corresponding city ordinance prohibiting women from "impersonating a man." This was a clear case of sexual discrimination, according to the judge. Yet, we accept these discriminations against men without question.

Raising a gay son

The truth is that parents can't cause a son to become homosexual even if they try. We don't know how to do it. If someone offered a woman twenty million dollars to raise a homosexual son, she wouldn't know how to do it. Nobody does.

But I hear both men and women expressing concern about sons. One feminist writer said of rearing her son: "I want to approach it as a liberal. But secretly I am glad he likes guns and tanks and to play fort with the kids in the neighborhood."

For all these pressures, there is regret on the part of some mothers for having pushed their sons to be tough little guys. Other mothers find themselves pushing their sons away emotionally so they won't be "mama's boys." Many young boys are pushed away by this fear.

Fathers, too, feel the pressure to make their sons tough. Unfortunately, when we get in too big a hurry to make sure our sons are rough and tough enough, we lose valuable bonding time. We lose time that could have been used as the foundation for a stronger, closer relationship.

Giving little boys more latitude for self-expression and by letting them show their emotions isn't going to create a bunch of wimps or softies who can't make it in the world. You cannot give a child, boy or girl, too much affection and support. Studies show that CEOs of major corporations and male leaders in all walks of life were usually smothered with love during their formative years. By enforcing rigid masculine expectations, parents do one thing: block the road to emotional maturity.

What is frustrating is that there is no evidence that forcing a young boy to be tough will create the Marlboro man, rugged type. What they will end up with is a silent type, a son who has difficulty opening up and embracing the full range of human emotions. A son who can't share with others ends up trusting no one and doubting himself.

CHAPTER THIRTEEN

A MESSAGE FROM THE GENTLE SEX

Question for women: Do you hold out a dual message to men, saying in one breath that you appreciate sensitivity, but reward men (even little boys) for being self-charging macho types?

We teach other people how to treat us. How we treat others and how we treat ourselves serve as a mirror. The actions are reflected back to us.

Before men and women reach a better understanding, they need to accept this as a basic truth. Each of us is a teacher. And it is up to each one to be an ambassador of change or a victim of the *status quo*.

Many of us have walked into a store feeling out of sorts and uncomfortable. Maybe it's an expensive gift shop and we wonder if we belong there. Often, the sales clerks will ignore you making you feel worse. They tend to walk over to the confident, happy shoppers. That is human nature, and it has little to do with whether or not you belong in the store. In most cases, you decide by your actions whether others accept your presence.

Present at the creation?

Sometimes I find myself wondering if I ever really learned The Code. Maybe I just inherited it along with the testosterone that men are supplied with at conception.

But that doesn't explain the thousands of stories I've heard from other men who seem to have learned their behavior, rather than simply having been invaded by funny little genes. Paradoxically, many of these men remember the gentle sex encouraging or rewarding early Code-like behavior.

Women as Code enforcers

A man who is now a successful health-care administrator, relates the following:

When I was little, my Dad did construction work and we traveled around a lot. During the time we lived in Detroit, I was the runt of the class and everybody picked on me. One day, after acquiring a hole in my pants from trying to run from one of my tormentors and falling, my Mother made me a proposition. She said she would give me a silver dollar if I would slug the next guy who picked on me. I did, came home with a black eye, and got my silver dollar.

He got something else. A clear message of how he was expected to handle difficulties from that time forward: by himself. As he explains:

My Mom still brags about how brave I was. But she has conveniently forgotten what he did to me. And while I love my Mother to death, the fact of the matter is, she never had to stand toe-to-toe with a guy a head taller than she was, mouth dry, legs shaking and fight it out, getting desperately hurt in the process.

At the time, I thought my Mother was sort of a "wicked witch" to make me fight. But I've since realized that she was only reflecting the attitudes I would encounter for the rest of my life. And I've learned to give them what they want. I don't pay much attention to the words people speak anymore, because they're usually said to make that person feel modern and liberated. Regardless of what people say, I innately know how I'm supposed to act, and that's what I do.

This story brings home an important point. Boys come to realize that they not only have to worry about other men, but that women are Code enforcers as well. While this story represents a direct effort on the mother's part to encourage her son to stand up and be tough, sometimes women nurture Code-like behavior inadvertently.

The more subtle enforcement

Recently, a mother of an eleven-year-old boy approached me during a workshop. She began to relay with obvious pride the story of how her boy was trying to act like a man. He didn't want a birthday party. He was "too old for childish parties and toys," he announced.

As we talked, she began to see the situation in a different light. "Do you really think your son is a man at age eleven?" I asked. "Does he really not want to play anymore? Is he trying to do the thing that will bring him admiration — and win your approval?"

After she weighed the questions, she reflected: "I thought it was so neat, him trying to act like a man. I see that we're rushing things a bit." She later told me, "It's funny how all of this stuff happens so unconsciously. How we push our sons into manhood."

Many times the subtle messages come from female peers. Penny, a physical education instructor in the public schools, shares the following insight:

Dear Dr. Towery:

I have been watching adolescents stumble from childhood into "adult" behavior for over ten years now. Since you write for men, I was wondering why young boys have to win, win, win. The girls in my classes rarely have that edge about them. They think they're cute when they fall down while trying to catch a softball. I have so few young women who I can coach in serious compe-tition because they're too busy noticing the boys. How do boys get the urge to compete, while so few girls want to push that hard?

Penny is on to something. It is *never* cute for a boy to miss a pass. No one gives him any attention or reward for failure — at anything. While cheerleaders are obviously rewarded for being physically adept and coordinated, any attractive girl can get just as much attention by pretending to not understand something, pretending to be "the world's worst softball player."

By comparison, no one applauds the young man who is all thumbs. When I was in high school, even the shyest of girls seemed to be attracted to the star basketball players or the varsity football players. They didn't seem very interested in the young chemistry whiz who forgot to tie his shoelaces, and walked with a slight shuffle.

At a very early age, boys receive the message loud and clear that the way to attract attention from the fairer sex is to win. So, in answer to the physical education teacher's question, boys receive the most praise, the most positive feedback from achievement, and hence the drive to win.

Hopefully, both sexes will learn a balance with young girls being praised more for autonomous achievement but not to the point where they become as worried about achieving for attention as young boys are. Similarly, it would be healthier if boys learned other avenues for being "heroes," instead of the limiting stereotype of the "hero jock."

There is evidence of change. One mom with a five-year-old daughter said she is seeing it in her own backyard. As she wrote to me:

Dear Dr. Towery:

My daughter's favorite playmate is young boy named Terry from across the street. They're both five years old. I think it's good for both of them.

Instead of always playing the same old games with dolls or trucks, these two have expanded their repertoire to include "pro-

ducing" a TV show, or running a hospital emergency room.

But my husband said if Terry's father finds out he is sticking with little girls all the time, he's really going to be upset. Not true. Things are changing. Terry's father came by the other day and mentioned that Terry's imagination was really expanding. He said he couldn't believe the games he was playing. He loved it! So ha! ha! to old macho ways.

How much change is enough?

Ironically, it seems to be women who so badly want men to exchange their Cro-Magnon personas. Don't many women want men to be more sensitive, able to cry, hug, and experience the joys of an encounter group held on soft cushions, shoes off, toes wiggling?

There's no doubt in my mind that the majority of women truly do want to see men change for the better. Sure, there are women out there who love perpetuating self-righteous feminist anger. But while loud, their numbers are relatively few. So why are women unwittingly part of the reason the antiquated Code remains?

For starters, they don't recognize the brute force of The Code. Women have been taught, particularly during the last half century, that people actually have a choice. That life is made up of certain options: Marry or focus on your career, work or be a homemaker, have children, or not. They don't believe that men are stamped by a Code that dictates their behavior in prescribed ways.

The trouble with feminist anger

Occasionally, I have met feminists who are so consumed with anger that the notion of equity is beyond their grasp. Once in a bookstore in Washington, D.C., I asked a woman to help me search for titles on the subject of mothers and sons. As she handed

me one text, she remarked that, "I know an excellent book, but
you probably won't be interested since it is printed by a feminist
publishing house."

As I leafed through the book she recommended, I wasn't
impressed with the presentation. It was clearly bogged down by
an extreme feminist viewpoint. When I asked what additional
titles she stocked on the subject of men, she said, "Why read
about men?" Intrigued, I asked if she had ever read books that
presented the other side of the coin. "No," she announced without
apology. "I'm not interested in being fair; I'm interested in re-
venge. Once we [women] get that, we can worry about being
fair."

It wasn't friendly anymore. This woman was serious. Not
only was I stunned, I was disappointed. In reading *The Sisterhood,* a well-balanced account of the women's movement by
Marcia Cohen, I was struck by the fact that up until 1964 employers could refuse competent women jobs — perfectly legally.[38] It
brought home exactly how young the women's movement is,
particularly from a historical perspective.

Cohen goes on to remind the reader that it wasn't long ago
that ads, such as, "Fly me, I'm Barbara," were acceptable. She
also reminds the reader of the "rage that smoldered in the feminist
heart," a rage that was bound to explode.[39]

But she goes one step better. She also is willing to say that
Betty Friedan, author of the landmark book, *The Feminine Mys-
tique,* damaged the movement with her manic, venomous attacks.
In the epilogue, she quotes Gloria Steinem's observation that the
" . . . New Left women say: 'I never had anything in my life.
Nobody else is going to have it either.' "[40]

Passionate conviction

On one level, "passionate conviction" sounds like pretty
neat stuff. But there's a telling lesson in Cohen's work: passionate
conviction can all too quickly lead to passionate subterfuge. No
one wins when we build trenches instead of bridges. We all need

to acknowledge that both sexes are in a stage of transition that will inevitably cause some pain for both sides.

In the "Acknowledgments" for their book, *Why Can't Men Open Up?*, authors Naifeh and Smith make a striking observation: "One of the surprises of this book was the hostility and ridicule heaped on the men's liberation movement by some women. We think the abuse is undeserved and self-indicting."[41]

Breaking out of stereotypes is as new to men as it is to women. And women who refuse to see this, such as the woman in Washington, do not perpetuate the women's movement — they diminish its spirit.

Understanding the chains

If women want men to change, they need to understand that there are chains that hold the man in place. They can ignore or ridicule them. But if they really want to see change, they must become involved in taking the shackles off.

When the burden of the masculine manifesto is never taken off his shoulders, that's when a man strikes out. When a woman rebuffs a man's attempts to change, or throws anger into the equation, it hurdles men back further into their macho cage. At least The Code is familiar territory. There is comfort in continuity, and these rules of behavior have been passed down by countless generations of men.

Unfortunately, the net result of feminist anger is the opposite of change. The anger triggers a defense against the "wimp factor." It's safer, and he can defend from within its stronghold. Almost as a knee-jerk reaction, a man simply becomes more entrenched in macho behaviors.

By comparison, one of the best ways to effect change is to not engage chauvinistic or macho behavior. Don't give it credibility through an argument. Show your surprise and even amusement at his archaic behavior or thinking.

That will throw the chauvinists of the world off-center. And that's what will make them change the most. Men hate to appear silly. To be laughed at is the greatest humiliation. When they are no longer given credence for their attitudes, they will let go of them.

CHAPTER FOURTEEN

HOW IT FEELS WHEN MEN
OPEN UP: KABOOM!

Question for men: *Do you think it is always best to err on the side of silence, and find yourself holding back sensitive information that might help others to understand you?*

When the "new man" opens up

Learning about each other is critical to healthy relationships in the work place and at home. As a columnist and speaker who addresses issues facing the modern male, I hear both sides of the transition.

I have often heard from men who try to be "new men," only to be shocked by the response from the "new women." Many of these men are devastated, for example, after they finally open up to a woman they love, only to watch her recoil both physically and emotionally. The following is one such example:

Dear Dr. Towery:

Recently something shattered me emotionally and makes no sense to me in light of what I keep hearing. Carolyn and I were in love and planning to marry. She is a manufacturer's rep for a large firm, makes good money, is independent, and believes open and completely honest communication is extremely important. The subject came up often, and she constantly urged me to become more open with her and share my feelings. Men should talk.

Men should cry. Men should express their love to each other. Men should discuss their fears.

Well, I finally did! I described to her an irrational, silly fear of mine emanating from a childhood incident and cried during the telling. I could not only feel, but literally see her physically spacing herself from me. And it's been that way ever since. She has avoided me. Our relationship is over.

I confronted her and she finally broke down and admitted that while she wasn't proud of her reaction, she simply couldn't handle my weak side. She said seeing me cry like a baby was repugnant to her and regardless of how it could be intellectualized, that's just the way it is.

What kind of liberation is this? Is this equality of the sexes? Is my case unique? Is this the way the "new woman" reacts to the "new man"?

Of course there are millions of women who would not have reacted as Carolyn did. In fact, many women would feel much better about their relationships if this kind of communication did take place.

Having said that, though, the fact remains that many women confide that they have reacted in much the same way. While not pleased with their response, it was how they honestly felt. These women still want a stronger shoulder than their own and are undone when male fears are expressed graphically.

Some books that many women read stress that men are basically programmed to be insensitive jerks. No mention is made of the programming of women to expect the unreal or the impossible of men; in short, that they will always be strong and able to successfully take charge when the going gets rough. To some women, the new equality really means drawing on all of the positives, but discounting the negatives.

The purpose here, however, is not to point to women as the source of the problem — only to say that women at times contribute to the cycle. As support, I refer to Jan Halper, who in one issue of *Cosmopolitan* magazine summarized her findings from interviews with over four thousand successful men, ranging in age from twenty-seven to seventy-eight.[42]

Close to 70 percent of the men in the study felt that women have a difficult time responding to a man's vulnerabilities. "Although many women I know encourage men to understand their feelings or even teach them how to do so, judging from the men's comments, that percentage of women is small," Halper writes. The majority of men found women were not willing to "be there" emotionally for them.

In fact, Halper let the president of a major motion-picture company sum up her findings: "You women think you want us to be more open, to show our feelings and be more sensitive, but that's not the case. Women clam up when we act that way. They don't really want us to show our feelings. They merely want us to understand theirs."[43]

That's too broad a generalization, but it remains a sore point for many men who do try to be the "new male" and open up. Many of the letters I receive address this issue. One husband writes of his attempt at letting down his guard:

Dear Dr. Towery:

The other night, I watched a TV program that had some woman author on talking about what "women want out of the new men," or something. I was about to turn if off, when my wife laughed and said that I should watch. So I did. This woman talked on and on about how women want men to open up and be gentle and all that, that they were leaving us like never before because we weren't.

I didn't think about it too much at the time, but I guess my wife was trying to give me a message.

About half a week later, I ran into an old friend of mine from high school, who is doing really well. Since I am not really satisfied with how my life has gone, it really upset me. When I went home, and my wife asked the standard, "What's wrong?" I did tell her, instead of being tough. I have to say that I broke down and cried to her, thinking that I should be more open with her. But when I did, she physically backed away! I mean, she tried to act nice about it, saying nice stuff, but I could see the look of . . . almost disgust on her face. Later she said nervously that I had to "toughen up about it." What's wrong? I thought she wanted me to be open and stuff!

The reader's decision to make an effort at change is right. However, when it comes to men changing themselves (so that they stop dying seven-and-a-half years before their mates), their efforts are not always met with unconditional acceptance.

Now it is his wife's turn to change. When the women's movement went into high gear, there was a lot of talk about how men were going to have to adjust to the "new woman." But there simply hasn't been much talk about women changing their expectations of or reactions to the "new man."

We know that men have a certain idea of how they are supposed to be that can be harmful to their well-being, i.e., The Code. Yet women often fail to support changes; in short, to respond positively to the new men. They may think intellectually that they want their husbands to open up, while still emotionally depending on them to be the strong, silent partner.

In the above case, it's also important to point out that gender traits are one thing, but communication is another. The reader and his wife may have a problem in communication that goes beyond any masculine/feminine concerns. He needs to ask himself how many other things he cannot talk about in front of his spouse, and address the issue with her, perhaps with the help of a counselor.

The double bind

In all fairness, women have a legitimate gripe when it comes to the emotional competence and communication skills of men. What they don't readily see is that they place men in a double bind.

As women move from one avant-garde therapy, support group, or strategy to another, they view men going nowhere. Or worse, they view men as being only a shadow of their ideal male, men such as their own father, brother — or a combination of male symbols such as Richard Gere, Clint Eastwood, and Alan Alda.

"Why can't I find men like that?" these women ask. "All I ever see are alcoholics, gays, married men on the make or mamma's boys." What a neat trick it would be to mix a cake of equal portions of the coldblooded Eastwood, the hypersensitive Alda and the enigmatic Gere. But would women have it? "Sure," answered one real estate broker, I interviewed, "but only one piece at a time."

So much is said about the impossible expectations we place on women: beautiful creature, responsible mother, work place equal, gourmet cook, uninhibited lover, career supporter, surrogate mother, stimulating conversationalist, and dozens more. No thinking person would deny that today's woman has complex roles to fulfill in her own right.

But often the same generous observer of the female plight ridicules the emotional obstacle course faced by men. After all, isn't it a man's world? Our pop psychology culture is inundated with messages of how women have been programmed to do this, coerced to do that. They don't apply the same logic to men, except to agree that men share a collective craziness.

Collective craziness

They're on to something here! Men do have a collective craziness, prompted by The Code's impossible model. And compounded by the double messages men continue to receive. One TV personality recently quipped that "even Hemingway couldn't be Hemingway!" He's right.

In terms of men's craziness, the male mid-life crisis is a case in point. It may be the source of a lot of jokes, but it's deadly serious stuff to the guy who suddenly finds that after doing all of the "have-tos," he nonetheless feels he is a "have-not."

And the end is in sight for him. When the morning sun showers his bedroom with light, a man in his forties starts to wonder if this is *the day*. He begins to reflect on all the time he has wasted. And doing what? For too many, life becomes a process of imitation — imitating the man he thinks he's supposed to be instead of following his inner dreams.

Too many times, he realizes, he has assumed a passive role, allowing life to act upon him, instead of the other way around. And for the first time, he can see the dark at the end of his tunnel, and knows he has limited time to make his life count.

His best friends — even his wife — are appalled. Puzzled. Angry. "We've got a beautiful home, two great kids, you've made vice president, we belong to the best club in town, and you start acting like a crazy man," the wife says.

Her timing's a little off. The crazy part was when he stepped into the school yard circle, with knees of jelly and shaking hands, to fight the bully amid the snarled screams of his classmates. Crazy was when he took geometry and physics when he wanted to study art and drama because his parents said he had to prepare himself in a practical way to make a good living in a tough world.

Crazy was when he dated the high school cheerleader who everybody thought was darling, instead of the girl in biology lab who made him laugh — all because everybody said she was a bookworm and had a big nose.

Crazy was playing football because that's what strong boys do, rather than play the piano after school, which gave him both an excitement and a calm like nothing else he knew. And a whole blur of crazy years were spent in graduate school, like his daddy and his daddy before him, when his soul ached instead to study sculpture.

And the end result was predictable. What he became over the years was haunted. He wore the masculine mask to perfection by denying his inner reality. The exterior was a facade that bore little resemblance to his core feelings.

Unfortunately, for a man, the facade of self-confidence — always appearing to be in control of his emotions — works as a suit of armor. After all, doesn't the majority of the population continue to say, "it's a man's world"? Someone's buying it.

Faking it

At least more women are coming forward to say they're tired of faking it. One female reader recently wrote:

Dear Dr. Towery:

I've got a pet peeve about men I want to air. They always expect me to be smiling. If I'm not smiling they want to know what's wrong. Why am I unhappy? Am I mad at them, and on and on. I don't always want to smile. Men don't always smile and nobody jumps on them. I've got friends who have the same problem, so I want your opinion about whether this is common or are we crazy?

Men are still taught that there is virtue in concealing and withholding emotions. Women are praised and pursued when they are expressive, theatrical, and open with their emotions. Strong silent type vs. Mary Poppins. In fact, one of the major hurdles men must overcome is their reluctance to release their emotions. It's a killer — literally.

In the above example, if one of the woman's male friends wants to know why she isn't smiling, she needs to level with him. Tell him her real feelings, whether she is hurt, or angry, or whatever the case may be.

It would also be helpful to go one step further and explain that when two people are good friends, it isn't necessary for one or the other to put on an act. Being yourself is the highest compliment you can give a real friend.

And in friendships, relationships or strong working partnerships, it needs to be a two-way street with both the man and the woman able to express their honest reactions. There is one caveat, however: in working relationships, diplomacy and tact are the watchwords, not total openness.

Eventually, more men and women will learn to transmit and receive clear messages from each other. Both have to do their part. There is no getting around it. Another woman wrote in to say that hanging in there is tough, but she is going to give it a try:

Dear Dr. Towery:

After one of your workshops I "set the table" for my husband to open up about his job. If you recall, he's been real moody and angry about something, and I assumed that it's his work.

I pried gently. Well, he let it spill out. I've never seen such emotion from him. He HATES his work. At first his actions scared me. I'm used to him always saying, "No problem." To be honest, I didn't want to hear that he wanted to quit working. But I remembered all the times he listened to me gripe about graduate school and then the times he held me when I couldn't stand things anymore at my job.

The tension is way down in our house. I am worried (a little) that he will quit his job before he finds another, but I think somehow we'll make it. He never quits believing in me, even when I get hysterical. I guess it's my turn to return the compliment.

Bravo! It is time and I know it wasn't easy. Change doesn't always feel good. No one will tell you it does. It takes patience and faith. It *may* get worse before it gets better. But nothing can beat the feeling that you've tried.

CHAPTER FIFTEEN

BREAKING THE CODE OF SILENCE

Question for women: When you try to reach out to a man, to discover his inner feelings, do you think he shuts you out? Is this particularly true when you are angry with him?

One of the most positive effects prompted by women's emotional openness — and their insistence that men share more of their emotional side — is that greater numbers of men are questioning the validity of a life behind closed doors.

As more women encourage men to shed the silent act, many men are realizing the healthy emotional gains of sharing their inner dreams, their secrets, their private thoughts. And they can do this not only with women, but with other men as well.

Prompting openness

For example, one woman I know changed jobs last year. An interior designer, she moved to a firm where the pace was more intense, and she began working on Saturdays to keep up. Already in her forties and married for twelve years, she assumed her workaholic husband would be delighted with the transition. "I thought he would be glad that I wouldn't expect him home on the weekends," she explained.

Instead, she began feeling a stony silence from her husband. She asked several times why his attitude had changed — why did he seem so angry at her? "We went through several rounds where he simply denied his anger," she says. "So I decided to handle the problem just like a corporate retreat. In other words, try some problem solving out of our usual environment. I ambushed him with tickets to his favorite golf resort, and he grudgingly consented to a long weekend."

She was surprised with her discovery. During their long weekend, her husband confessed to wanting to slow down. "Now I just feel more pressure to keep on the merry-go-round I started," he said. "It's like we're on two different trains. Just when I was ready to take your advice and start spending more time at home on the weekends, you go off in a different direction. "I could never have guessed his intentions," she now says. "I was beginning to think he hated me — that no matter what I did it was a step in the wrong direction. I prefer to play on the weekends. It just took some digging to find out that we were moving closer, not further apart."

More ways than one

Can a woman break through the Code of Silence? Yes. And there are several different ways to do it. One of the easiest ways is to set the table, so to speak, for meaningful conversation. A woman can let her partner know up front what her intentions are — that she is tired of being shut out, and she isn't going to stand for it anymore.

I know what you're thinking. That's probably good for a grunt from the beast. But it takes time to set the table. Start by sharing your own private thoughts. If that gets you nowhere, ask your husband to make a list of the most important things that happened to him during the week. Share them. Make it a game, as if the two of you are sitting down to play Trivial Pursuit. You'll be surprised at how much the list will tell. And how much you didn't know!

Keep up the list for at least a month, longer if you think it continues to shed new light. After a while, a pattern of sharing is set up that can continue with or without the written list.

A commitment to open up

What many men lack, because of the Code of Silence, is a genuine commitment — not in their chosen line of work, but in terms of personal growth. Because of their fear of losing emotional control, men avoid emotional risks. Being open, for example, means a man might be "found out"; his flaws might be examined. It takes courage and strength to take that risk. As one thirty-five-year-old computer software programmer confessed:

It took me a long time to realize that the more cowardly thing to do is to keep everything inside. Yeah, I've heard women like the strong, silent types, and I know from experience that many do. But not the healthy women. They know that those silent guys are grinding inside. It's unhealthy and eventually spells trouble. If a woman can't see that, I don't need her.

His point is well-taken. Not surprisingly, the programmer reported that he is happily married. Men need to learn that rules need to be evaluated by their results. And The Code is no exception.

In the latter part of *The Good Girl Syndrome,* the authors ask: How do you know when you are breaking out of old, counterproductive habits? The answer is when you are more interested in seeing results from your efforts than paying homage to old systems.[44]

For men, opening up is comparable to cliff walking. It doesn't feel natural or safe. They must feel rewarded for this behavior. Like the computer programmer, goal-oriented men will open up more as they find women who value this trait.

Will they ever be as open and expressive as women? Not any time soon. And counting on dramatic change is one of women's greatest mistakes in relating to men. The following letter illustrates my point:

Dear Dr. Towery:

Jed and I plan to get married but we've got one big problem — he won't open his feelings up to me. It hurts me. If he can't trust me, who can he trust? Is he likely to change?

Jed is not likely to become openly expressive. In fact, many men who are quite verbal during the unnatural and highly emotion-charged courtship stage revert to their "normal" self after marriage and clam up again. Women need to accept that the Jeds of the world simply aren't at ease telling anybody, including their partners, about their weaknesses. Or, talking about what they *perceive* as their weaknesses. Remember, it has been grilled into them before they had a vocabulary that showing feelings *is* weakness.

It's important to understand that Jed, like most men, is afraid to tell his dreams and ambitions, because he's afraid he won't achieve them — and then the people he cares about the most will think less of him. He is sure he will be considered a "failure." He will be laughed at.

It is important to show men that communication is valued, not performance. Love, not accomplishment. Men will assuredly be silent until they can trust that their efforts will be valued, particularly by women. When men know, through experience, that affection is unconditional and not based on them "doing" anything, then, and only then, will they say what is in their heart.

Confronting the facades

The men who are willing to confront their ghosts — or their facades — learn that their kind of socialization has in many ways isolated them. A man's feelings are often boiling beneath the surface, waiting for appropriate expression — or an inappropriate explosion. As the emotional side smolders, men do start acting crazy, many times in a self-destructive manner through aggression, addiction, or by retreating, like the man in the above example.

It's important to keep in mind that the male's traditional

silence in no way signifies lack of feelings. What operates over-time in the male's psyche is a fear of his own vulnerability. He's undoubtedly spent a lifetime (or so it feels) trying to avoid being labeled a "pussy."

Why men don't deal well with anger

In a similar way, the male is afraid of his own emotional volatility, which causes him to bury his anger deeper — or at least to try. This is the reason many women complain that their male partners are incapable of a "healthy fight." Many of the letters I receive deal with this issue:

Dear Dr. Towery:

My husband, Mark, is infuriating. He is so unromantic, in the sense he never goes out of his way to make me feel special. I don't want to give just one side, so I must admit he's a good husband in his own way. He's strong and he takes care of things.

But every time I confront him about his lack of romantic feelings, he pulls away and gives me the silent treatment. No matter what I say to him, no matter how insulting I get, I get the same response. He fixes himself a drink and then goes off and putters — repairs a window, or some appliance, or something. I can't even get him to get mad! I've heard that the opposite of love is ambivalence, and it bothers me that he never even has any anger towards me. Does that mean a man doesn't love a woman?

A man's inability to deal with anger in a healthy fashion rarely has anything to do with his lack of love or lack of feelings. While the wife may assume Mark doesn't have strong feelings for her because he "walks away" from a sparring match, it might mean quite the opposite. For him, not engaging in a fight might be the way he expresses his caring.

Most men grow up with the idea that women are to be protected, not abused verbally and certainly not physically. If a man is afraid of his temper — the volatility of his own well of anger — he might well flee the fight to avoid being pushed too far.

Unfortunately, this is a great source of frustration for many women. From the male perspective, the woman's insistence on a good fight can create an ongoing tension that men have difficulty dealing with. The following letter from a troubled husband illustrates my point:

Dear Dr. Towery:

I don't understand my wife. Jill is sweet and gentle 98 percent of the time. But when I do something to upset her, she's the worst tiger imaginable. We've only been married two years, and I've already taken to leaving the apartment when she is in one of her moods.

The trouble is, she stews and just gets madder at me. How can I explain to her that I don't want to scream and yell at her? She thinks I'm rotten for walking out. How can I get through to her?

The above letter reflects a common problem for men. It is very difficult to explain the different fighting styles of men and women. Men, for the most part, retreat from a woman's hostility. They don't know how to deal with it.

Remember, fighting for them means winning. As boys, men are taught to beat their adversary to reaffirm their manhood. To let out all the stops. Do whatever it takes. Go for the jugular. By the same token, they're taught early on not to use brute strength on girls. As they mature and do things to anger the women in their lives, they have difficulty finding the right outlet. They're stumped. They are afraid that once they get started they won't be able to stop until after they have seriously, maybe fatally, hurt the one they love. Usually, they retreat because they *do* care.

Redefining masculine behavior

The issue of anger aside, there is a growing number of men willing to listen more closely to their own conscience. A call for change is in the air. Men are more willing to define for themselves what feels right and what is natural for them, regardless of The Code's spell. And regardless of what women want.

In writing about how men try to adapt to women in their lives, Dr. Warren Farrell, in *Why Men Are the Way They Are,* captures the paradox men try, but cannot live by.[45] "We have seen how this performing makes men successful in attracting women and unsuccessful with the women they attract. So men are torn: what we did to *get* intimacy is the opposite of what it takes to *have* intimacy."

Many men are tired of the paradox. They are tired of old rules that promise nothing more than a shallow victory on their masculine scorecard. Not long ago, one man wrote:

Dear Dr. Towery:

I am a businessman, but I don't really like being one. It seems like everyone I work around, women and men alike, are totally involved in work and career. They will work any night or weekend, travel any amount, and do anything to get ahead.

There are other things I would rather do. I hate the cutthroat methods of American business. I don't blame the system. I'm just worried that something is wrong with me. I've done well, but lately I literally feel like throwing up before I get to work. Do other men feel this way?

Many men have similar feelings. What's more, many people who seem so happy and self-assured in reality share this man's feelings and doubts.

It's interesting to note that the person did not question the system. Instead, he worried that something was wrong with him. Isn't it possible, even likely, that the reverse is true? It's time for men to stop berating themselves, to realize the deck is stacked, demand a new deck, and start a whole new game.

This man made an important first step in exorcising his own haunted feelings. To effectively break out of the cycle, however, both men and women must acknowledge that a stringent and often unlivable Code really does exist. It takes an act of faith. Both must believe.

Then, women can stop pointing fingers at men, and men at themselves.

CHAPTER SIXTEEN

FROM THE MAGIC OF
BOYHOOD FRIENDSHIPS

*Question for men: Do you find yourself looking back at your
childhood and reminiscing about the magical
closeness of boyhood friendships?*

Adult friendships for men are often dim reflections of the
almost magical intimacy they shared with their boyhood friends
— long before they became serious competitors. Donald H. Bell,
author of *Being a Man, the Paradox of Masculinity,* observes that
as adults, men seem to lose the capacity to sustain close friendships, and many of us end up looking back with nostalgia to a
time when we could be intimate with male peers.[46]

It's an excellent point because the majority of men operate
as emotional islands by their late twenties. Information is viewed
as a potent weapon, rarely to be shared with other people. The
Code also dictates that a man always act in control: there's no
leeway for telling a "best buddy" that you might have a drinking
problem, or you just know the IRS is going to get you. No way.
The buddy might think you're weak. He might think you're incapable of handling your drinking problem on your own. So this
"good buddy" then might feel a need to mention your "drinking
problem" to your boss. All in your best interest, of course. "Gee,
I bet this extra drinking he's been doing lately is just a passing
thing, don't you?"

How the male bond changes from childhood

For a man, some of the happiest times of his life were when he shared his innermost secrets with a childhood friend. For young boys this takes on the aura of a great adventure. As we built play forts or sneaked out together at night to go fishing, we became best buddies, blood brothers, two against the world. There was complete trust, and it felt *wonderful*.

Before a boy's age hits a double digit, these secret bonds have incredible impact. Typically, it involves rituals and a swearing of fealty — a compelling oath of allegiance to the friendship. The issue of loyalty is of paramount importance.

One of my female friends, for instance, remembers a long day from her childhood when she unwittingly "betrayed" her brother. Her eight-year-old brother was going to fight a boy of the same age whose family had recently moved into the neighborhood. She wasn't sure who she was going to cheer for, since the new neighbor intrigued her and she liked him a great deal.

Her brother was furious; she knew she had done serious damage to her brother's trust. He interpreted her failure to side with him as betrayal. She still remembers her brother glaring at her over lunch as though she were the lowest form of life. To him, at that moment, she was.

Still best buddies in the teens

As men hit their teens, their buddies still surround them. Basically, anyone who isn't one of their buddies is on the outside — the enemy. The mentality that goes with these bondings is that you are either with me or against me.

Even as they enter college and join fraternities, the male rituals continue and so do the secret oaths. The fraternity represents a complete identity for many of these young men. If you know so-and-so is a Deke, well, you can pretty much sum up who he is, what he stands for. The fraternal affiliation presents a strong, tangible personality of its own.

A friend of mine, who is a university professor, tells me that his male graduate students love it when I speak to his classes, because it allows them once again to talk about what they legitimately need and miss: male friends. One interesting observation that my friend makes is that many of these men say that their last intimate male experience was the fraternity in their undergraduate days.

At the end of most fraternity meetings comes the equivalent of a "truth" session when anyone can say anything and everyone is bound to secrecy. Men generally have no mechanism to replace this vital process once the fraternity experience ends. Even today, when I face a personal problem of great impact, I'm likely to pick up the phone to reach a friend from my fraternity past of more than twenty years ago.

Street gangs are also a strong, although misguided, form of male adolescent bonding. Loyalty is still of primary importance and is tied up with the notion that you're willing to go down with your buddies for the group's cause. As The Code says, "you take care of your own." Nothing has greater import than the fraternal web.

But "web" is a good word because these bonds are tenuous, often based on picking common enemies and rallying for a fight. When these boys begin to take strides to establish their own individuality, the web begins to dissolve. As they enter their early twenties and start pursuing a career or starting a family, they have for all practical purposes broken the tenuous threads of the male bond.

The broken bond

The stage is now set for less intimate "friendships" with men. While the young boy has realized all along that other boys were his competitors, by his mid-twenties he has to define his own turf, his own worth.

As he enters the job market or perhaps begins a family, his primary role is that of breadwinner. He either takes the bread home, or another guy does. The buddies of his boyhood cannot really help him do this. The burdens loom larger, and he —and he alone — is the only one who is going to carve his mark on the world.

Oh, he may have a group of softball buddies or bowling pals. He may even invite the guys over for a game of poker every Friday night. But something has changed. Sharing secrets is *verboten*. So the ritualistic behavior of his adolescent past may continue through the Friday night group, or the best foursome ever, but the notion of trust has been lost along the way.

The same guy who told Fred at fourteen about his first night with a girl wouldn't dream of telling Fred at twenty-eight that he had his first spell of impotence. And if he and Fred were going to conquer the world together at fourteen, by their twenties, they feel that they must conquer it separately — and possibly dominate each other in the process. The rules of The Code are unspoken, but all men know them.

Somewhere in their late teens, men walk off an emotional cliff that prevents them from bonding. As mentioned earlier, competition is one of the key factors affecting the change, since it generally has reached an acute level by the time men have passed through their teenage years. In other words, if as a boy he might have helped Fred pass a math exam, he holds no rosy illusions as an adult: If he helps Fred look too good now, Fred may end up with his job or his seat on the board.

The fear of homophobia

A second factor starts coming into play — homophobia. A boyhood hug or the sexual exchanges that most adolescent boys experience at one time or another become totally taboo as early as thirteen or fourteen years of age.

The reason is simple. By the age of fourteen, boys are hit with an almost universal experience: he is "caught" hugging a pal, or walking arm in arm with a teammate. Typically, it is an older boy who yells, "Look at the queers!" In the throes of his adolescence, he freezes inside, and starts to operate defensively.

Suddenly, all physical gestures, with the exception of rough slaps or mock punches, begin to fall into the domain of homosexuality. Without arguing for or against homosexual practices here, the point is most men would rather die than be called a "queer." To a man, this is even worse than being called a woman, or a "pussy."

At this point, it becomes "natural" for young adolescents to begin to criticize "homo" activity in their peers. They watch for affection and denounce it with the least provocation. The ones most vocal in their denunciations are often the boys most afraid to explore the urge for male intimacy. Sometimes battling latent homosexuality in themselves, these are the boys who take a macho stance against homosexuals, embodied in such cruel phrases as: "If a queer touches me, I'll kill the summbitch!"

Rewards for calm, collected behavior

A third factor begins to enter the picture. By his late teens, a boy begins to receive conflicting messages concerning his aggressive, boisterous behavior. While he was praised as a youngster for enjoying rough contact sports and being physically aggressive, suddenly he starts hearing the message that calm, cold, collected behavior will make him more effective in the work place.

Again, the change is like walking off a cliff. At twelve, he hears: "If Fred takes your ball, it's up to you to beat him up and teach him a lesson." When he is twenty, the rules have changed. Now, he is supposed to beat Fred up with facts and figures in order to get his own way — no more physical rough stuff. But rough stuff, nonetheless.

The boisterous, high-contact antics of his childhood meld into the realm of the taboo. In a more subtle form, it's the same painful, double message we give to war veterans. In one breath, society announces, "Go out and give 'em hell. Kill all the sons a bitches you can!"

But what happens when the soldier comes home? We ask him to be a gentleman; be calm; don't overreact. It's a tall order for any human being to reconcile those two messages, and it's no wonder that many men feel caught in an emotional catch-22 — especially at the age of twenty.

Working through the barriers

In order to work through The Code messages that prevent men from forming genuine friendships, it is necessary for a man to admit that many of his adult friendships operate on a superficial level.

While the majority of men freely admit that they lack close male friends, there are still a number who think their buddies will always be there for them — and they're adamant on the subject. Undoubtedly, these men do have friends, but they have rarely put them to the test. As one reader painfully confided:

Dear Dr. Towery:

I am in my fifties, married with two grown children. I have been a good family man and good company man. But my wife has a serious illness that has wiped us out financially. I could live with that. What I have trouble with is that my best men friends are acting like I've done something wrong. They avoid me. These are the same guys I've worked with for ten or more years, golfed with, got drunk with. Raised hell. But now I'm treated like I'm contagious. Why in the world am I suddenly "diseased" in their eyes?

The man is definitely not "diseased," but he is experiencing a common problem with adult male friendships. All too often the friendships are based on a commonality of interests or work.

If you're down, other men don't know how to respond. You might become "mushy" — "a girl," as they say. I suspect most of this man's friends would like to help, but they haven't been trained to connect with feelings. Quite the opposite. In short, they are afraid to deal with his potential emotional volatility in light of his wife's illness and his financial difficulties.

This man understands the tenuous ties of most male friendships. He is living it, and it hurts.

Writing about it is a healthy first step. It is also helpful to talk to an objective third party about your difficulties, be it a rabbi, minister, social worker or therapist. They can help to keep things in perspective, and they are skilled at helping people through difficult times.

One of the most effective methods is to try sharing feelings with male friends on an ongoing basis. Don't wait until disaster strikes.

For example, call when you want to talk about how great you feel since you bought your new exercise machine. Try calling when you feel a little down because the boss is considering another man for a promotion. Test the waters slowly. Help your friends become better friends by allowing them to express their emotions as well.

CHAPTER SEVENTEEN

THE ENIGMA THAT FAILS

Question for women: Do you think men in the work place are always willing to help another man (their buddies) but not a woman? And do you also think men relax and let their guard down around each other?

Women often express the idea that men have a very close and valuable network of friends. Women often complain to me that men have a great system in place to help each other. It is usually labeled the "good ole boy" network. But regardless of the label, it is an enigma.

Men are as busy faking it in their friendships as in any other facets of their lives. Few people know the darker corners in men's hearts, because men themselves deny their existence. In his famous poem, "Richard Cory," Edwin Arlington Robinson dramatizes the difference between perception and reality:

Whenever Richard Cory went down town,
We people on the pavement looked at him:
He was a gentleman from sole to crown,
Clean favored, and imperially slim.

And he was always quietly arrayed,
And he was always human when he talked;
But still he fluttered pulses when he said,
"Good-morning," and he glittered when he walked.

And he was rich — yes, richer than a king —
And admirably schooled in every grace:
In fine, we thought that he was everything
To make us wish that we were in his place.

So on we worked, and waited for the light,
And went without the meat, and cursed the bread;
And Richard Cory, one calm summer night,
Went home and put a bullet through his head.
— *Edwin Arlington Robinson*[47]

The haunted, obviously unknown Cory, marched home the envy of the town to commit the final act of desperation: suicide. Evidently, no one knew that the man who had it all was tortured inside.

There is an uneasy parallel in the modern male's facade of bravado that is reminiscent of Richard Cory. By the time a man reaches his mid-twenties, The Code has been completely internalized.

Its effect is almost nova-like in its intensity. Like the nova that emits a brighter light for a few months or years, the male's act of bravado increases its intensity, but his core begins to fade. No matter what the cost, feelings of doubt, anxiety, and pain are kept inside.

Historically, men have equated emotionalism with weakness. They still do. In essence, it is the feminine domicile. Men endure; "pussies" weep.

The three-pad man

Ironically, feminist Gloria Steinem captured this sense of machismo well when she hypothesized about what men would do if they menstruated. She suggests that men, unlike women, would brag, "I'm a three-pad man," or "Yeah, man, I'm on the rag."[48] She's absolutely right. No room here for the embarrassing stuff.

The unflagging hero and friendship

Regardless of the day's experiences, men are expected to be packed with confidence. Nothing conquers the unflagging hero who lives and dies by The Code. And nowhere is this stereotype played out with more vengeance than in male friendships.

What happens if Tim loses an important client? His best friend, Joe, responds: "Cheer up. You'll get the next one." Or if his girlfriend suddenly leaves him, Joe may offer real solace: "Don't sweat it . . . So many women, so little time."

Forget the fact that Tim loves this woman and feels she is the best thing that ever happened to him. Feelings are not shared between men — they are buried. The haunted male is taught that there is virtue in concealing and withholding emotions. To give another human being personal information is to provide them with a weapon. Women, by comparison, are praised and pursued when they are expressive.

But women also tend to assume that men have the same latitude to express themselves — that they share all with their buddies. For instance, one woman wrote in:

Dear Dr. Towery:
I can't believe the way you go on about men being boxed in emotionally. Every time I go with my husband to the bowling alley to watch him play, I can't help but notice the way the guys all have fun. They always seem to be in a great mood. They joke, rib each other, and never seem to gripe about anything.

I'm jealous! When I get together with a group of women, we gossip. We get depressed more often than not, and don't seem to have the men's ability to just party.

The wife's description of her husband's bowling nights is more telling than she might at first realize. Sure, the guys joke around. That's because they're trained to keep sad or depressing thoughts to themselves. I can promise this woman that only some of those men feel like having fun partying when they go bowling.

In reality, one of the men may have learned that his three-year-old son has a learning disability. But he won't be able to let his guard down and share his problem. Another man may know his job is in jeopardy, but he won't be able to let his teammates see his fear.

Why men hide alone

Men, as a rule, think they are alone in their thoughts. Coupled with that is the fear that if others knew their private thoughts, they would judge them weak, unmanly. It is one of the reasons men often fail to complete the grieving process that women seem to glide through so adeptly. When you see things in win/lose terms, a loss often converts to a personal failure.

Because they are rarely able to share intimate thoughts or fears, it is no surprise that it takes men years longer to recover from traumatic events such as divorce or a death. While many women think men are the ones better able to put a relationship behind them, that is simply not the case. A man may *appear* to walk away with less bruises, but it's just a tough-guy response that reveals little of his inner turmoil.

The truth is, men are more emotionally dependent on women than vice versa. Although women might not see it, husbands usually view their spouse as their touchstone — their strongest connection to the world of emotions. It makes sense. Men are reared by women and are typically taught by women up through high school. To the little boy still inside, women are the center of the universe.

Divorced men, not surprisingly, are likely to suffer more severe depression, succumb to heavier use of alcohol and drugs, or to behave irrationally. "One of my best male friends," says one woman lawyer I interviewed, "went totally off the deep end in the year following his divorce. He grew long hair, stopped wearing suits, and took up race car driving. He drank like a fish, threw marathon parties, and ended up losing his job. It wasn't until after several years of therapy, and finally a new marriage, that his personality had any semblance of his former self."

The following letter from a young woman exemplifies the trauma many men experience following the breakup of a marriage or relationship:

Dear Dr. Towery:

I dated my old boyfriend for three years. We grew very close, and I have remained friends with many of the old group. I am writing because I am worried about my old beau, Jeff. I have a new relationship, but Jeff seems like a ghost. He doesn't want to hang out with anybody or do anything. It's been over a year since we broke up, and I think it's time for him to get on with his life. What can I do to help? I still care about him a lot.

It is painful to watch a man withdraw. Many times men do take longer to bounce back from a relationship because they can't share their feelings, their sense of loss.

As I suggested to the young woman above, one of the most positive steps friends can take is to make sure the person knows he is important to you, that you care about his feelings and friendship. Although it takes time, and the man may never talk about his feelings, just knowing friends are there for him can alleviate the more painful aspects of the healing process.

Jeff is probably unusual in that many men take great care to hide their sense of loss. They may take the opposite approach and strut around each weekend with a new honey — or boast to friends about how good it feels to be free. Nonetheless, they hurt inside.

Keeping up the enigma

There is a basic fear operating in men that to reveal all would be disastrous. To be enigmatic, remember, is a primary virtue, according to The Code. Not only could others use the knowledge against you, but would see you are nothing special if they got to view the whole package.

"People would be disappointed if they could look inside," is the way the typical man feels. And this fosters the need to be secretive, enigmatic — to always act like there is something just below the surface that others can't quite get to. Men try to live with their lies in fear that they will be found out and then no longer be wanted or loved.

In this regard, men can begin exhibiting characteristics of the impostor phenomenon. If one of these men receives kudos for being a financial wizard, an ingenious marketing man, or the best engineer, he inevitably wonders if it's really true. There's a lingering fear that he might not be *that* good — or worse, a new man will come on the job tomorrow who will lay all his efforts to waste and show him up as the mediocre jerk he always feared he was.

Try a little humor

In a humorous vein, one manufacturing executive opened up in a workshop and shared the following story:

I keep waiting for management to figure out that I don't know what I'm doing. I've only been with the company four years, and they've promoted me to executive vice president in charge of marketing. What a joke. I didn't even study business in college.

It's funny the number of days I sit in my office waiting for the walls to collapse around me — for an officer of the company to walk in and say, "Harry, WE KNOW. You don't know a thing about marketing, about manufacturing, about any of this stuff." But then I laugh, and think the only thing more frightening is that it's taken management this long to figure it out!

While this man obviously has a good sense of humor and can take things in stride, he relays a very common fear. Many men fear that they have been promoted beyond their level of competence. The difficulty for these men is that they never learn to talk or laugh about it.

There is an important lesson in Harry's sense of humor: Don't take yourself too seriously. Keep your work in perspective. Most of us aren't bulletproof, mistake-proof experts in what we attempt to do. Unfortunately, many men think they are alone in their enigmas. They are not. If they could look around and see inside others, they would see that they are in good company.

CHAPTER EIGHTEEN

THE FRATERNITY THAT ISN'T

Question for men: *Do you find yourself withholding important information from your male friends because you think they rely on you to be upbeat — no matter what?*

Many women mistakenly assume that there is a strong fraternity among men. The reverse is true because the first rule of The Code is to compete and win. Under close scrutiny, the male bond is a myth. The truth is, there are a number of men who refuse to admit that most of their friendships are based on superficial ties or confident posturing.

Where have you gone, Butch and Sundance?

The type of male friendship modeled in the movie, "Butch Cassidy & the Sundance Kid," has not disappeared, it just never existed — at least not in our culture. With few exceptions, men don't have close male friends.

Is there one friend they can turn to in their darker hours? "Perhaps my older brother," is the typical response. The notion of calling another man "just to talk things through" is alien to most of them.

What they do have, often in abundance, is acquaintances. Men are generally goal-oriented, so their male acquaintances are people they do things with: hunt, watch football, drink, or they talk over politics together. In short, men utilize each other to accomplish a specific goal.

139

Generally speaking, however, men do not see this trait in themselves. They think they are genuinely communicating with each other, as the following letter reflects:

Dear Dr. Towery:

You seem to think men don't talk much to each other, but that's not the case with me and my friends. We duck hunt and bass fish together regularly, staying at a camp together several week-ends per year. There are a lot of guys out there who do stuff together, whether it be hunting, playing softball or drinking beer, so give us a break.

These trips do represent time spent together. However, topics for discussion are typically limited to sports, philosophy, women, money or politics. Jokes are told, brags made, bets wagered, booze is consumed, and a lot of bull is given and received by all. These are what I call "car wax conversations," which only touch upon the superficial facts; they seldom tap real feelings, much less anxieties or problems.

These outings are usually fun. Also, they are generally the only avenue open for men to try to recapture some of the male intimacy they once had and always need. But the aloneness of men is never more apparent than on these trips.

The Code warns against revelations

Can you imagine a man on one of these excursions saying that he's afraid his problem with premature ejaculation might cause his wife to seek out a lover? Anybody ever speak up while sitting around the fire about waking up in the middle of the night, heart pounding, sweat dripping, afraid of having a heart attack — three times a week. Probably not.

The Code warns against such personal revelations, so the conversations seldom reach any real level of intimacy. Health worries, career fears, sexual problems, or any expressions of the anger and anxiety we all possess remain "safely" locked inside.

However, if a man could break through the barriers and share a personal dilemma, another man might have the opportunity to say, "I used to pop up in the middle of the night in a cold sweat and it scared the hell out of me, till I realized I was having a lot of anxiety about my son's drug problem. A therapist helped me work through it, and it doesn't happen any more. Let me give you his name. I bet he can get you over your anxiety, too." That's the kind of friendship men need, but don't get.

Psychologist Sharon Brehm describes the style of male friendships as "side by side" versus the women's preference for "face-to-face" friendships. What she means is that men are more inclined to sit in the bleachers and cheer or gripe together. Women, on the other hand, are more likely to sit over coffee and emotionally ventilate. The male style of friendship is based on shared histories or experiences, while the female style hinges on personal disclosure — at a level that astounds most men.[49]

The male version may be a millimeter better than being alone; but friendship it is not. Friendship for men is an outlet to play racquetball or drink beer rather than a bridge to share intuitive feelings. Among my bird-hunting buddies, for example, I've heard them jokingly remark about another man: "Don't go bird hunting with Homer. He'll have you contemplating the meaning of life — his life." The implication is clear. They may as well be saying: "Don't go hunting with this guy. He'll sit down and start knitting in the woods!"

And I've seen the pattern repeating itself time and again in male friendships. What do I mean? The following example illustrates my point:

The story of Frank, Byron, Trent, and Paul

Frank, Byron, Trent, and Paul became friends in their late twenties because of a mutual fondness for golf. Soon, they were traveling to other country clubs on weekends to enter invitational tournaments. They laughed, drank, told dirty jokes, gossiped. But mostly, they talked about golf: the best clubs, most challenging courses, correct grips.

After eight years of these shared experiences, Paul got a divorce. It shocked everyone, but nobody said much about it. After all, once it became common knowledge that Paul's wife had been involved with the lawyer she worked for and planned to marry him, nobody would dare bring up the subject to Paul. Too embarrassing for Paul.

Besides, ol' Paul was doing fine for himself, thank you. They all heard periodic reports of Paul being observed with one pretty young thing or another. In fact, they started calling him "Pussy Paul," and he smiled appropriately.

After a golfing trip to a Florida club where the drinking and merrymaking was particularly "fun," they returned home and went their own way.

Then Paul hanged himself.

He was found hanging from the basketball goal where he and his son Tommy often played before the divorce, after which Tommy disappeared with his mother.

The note addressed to Frank, Byron, and Trent, said: "With my family gone, you guys were my only friends. Sorry to do this, but I can't go on. Maybe one day you'll understand why I couldn't go on being alone. I need someone to talk to. Maybe God will talk to me."

The guys were hurt and angry. What does he mean, *talk*? We talked all the time. As Frank put it, "We tried to keep his mind off his troubles. Sometimes he would bring up his kid or his ex-wife, and we would get him off the subject as quickly as possible. We knew it was embarrassing for him."

No: It was embarrassing for Frank, Byron, and Trent. And it was trouble. It didn't meet the criteria set for their group performance many years earlier.

Paul needed to become personal, close, and intimate. But his "friends" wanted him to deal with his problems in private.

The surviving "Three Musketeers" became uncomfortable. While their wives openly cried and hurt, the men quivered alone in their thoughts. After the funeral, they got away from each other quickly, and their golf brotherhood slowly but purposefully disintegrated. They knew what they had done.

But more than hurt for Paul, they suffered for themselves. They suddenly realized their male "friendships" were alive only as long as they behaved confidently, made jokes, and appeared secure. But what about when trouble comes? And life does inevitably bring trouble. Who to turn to? Another man? And get pitied and rejected? "No sirree, buddy. I'll hack it alone."

Sharing is for the best of times

Unfortunately, in the world governed by The Code, friendships are for sharing success, stability, competition and kidding each other. Any true personal knowledge of each other is often discovered almost by accident, read between the lines, or most often, learned from gossip. The order of the day is to be happy, upbeat, positive, successful, and resilient. Little room here for divorce, illness, being fired, going bankrupt or making a fool of yourself over loving some woman.

Events such as these may not end a male friendship, but if you let these tests of your manhood change how you act and what you say — well, you obviously never belonged in the group in the first place. You haven't learned The Code. After all, Dirty Harry handles his problems in silence, and if he suffers any wounds, he licks them in private.

A tale from Vietnam

In our society, male camaraderie and male competition inevitably collide. The lack of personal exchange between men centers on two perceptions: (1) that other men are their competitors; and (2) that other men use information for leverage.

As I began working with men in seminars and workshops, I confirmed over and over again that they viewed competition as a pivotal factor in their lives. "I'm always looking at other men in terms of which one is going to stomp me into the floor," one tax lawyer confided. He laughed loudly during the telling, but the implication was clear: You don't let your competitors inside.

When and if men do communicate with any degree of intimacy, it is usually under circumstances of great duress, such as a critical illness or in times of war. Men settle for a vague sense of camaraderie, while women choose for intimacy, according to one Vietnam veteran I interviewed. The former Marine now living in Boston, Massachusetts, also shares this on the war:

The four of us were to spend a month on an outpost in Da Nang. Two guys from Texas, a tough New Jersey street kid, and a Bostonian. Only in a war.

One night I had the midnight to six watch with Johnny Lee from Texas. A real Texan. That night we told each other everything. It was the first time he or I ever had done it. We were nineteen. We were Marines for Christ's sake.

We told about lies to our girlfriends. Every shitty trick we had pulled in our lives up to that time. I told this guy about the first time I had ever got any. The woman was in her late thirties, married with three kids. She seduced me. It was the main reason I never went into the priesthood. It totally freaked me out. I told him I didn't get an erection for three years.

Then, Johnny told me about a girl he got pregnant and left behind. That's why he had joined the Marine Corps. We thought our secrets were the worst of the worst.

"The only reason we told each other those things," he confided during our interview, "is because we knew that neither of us knew anyone in the States to tell. And there was an attitude about life that we might never see that person again after that experience."

The war setting provided a certain freedom and trust. As he notes, "We were in a safety zone where we wouldn't be threatened. You knew the information wasn't going to be held over you." Even so, he recalls, the scene felt carefully orchestrated:

He told one secret; I told another. It was almost choreo-graphed, as I look back on it. We only revealed one card at a time, and the thing was, you never knew if it was going to be the six of hearts or the ten of diamonds. But we probably shuffled our cards around so that the twos came out before the jacks. In a way, it was sort of like playing poker. We both sensed the risk factor.

They learned this behavior as a boy, when their achievements were constantly being monitored and often harshly compared with those of other little boys. In the process, the other boys became competitors.

To be a man

Little boys are also painfully aware of the possibility of being made fun of by "the group." The tax lawyer, who went away to a boarding school at a young age, relays the following insight:

I can't remember when I wasn't facing this whole thing of not being a real man — it starts at such an early age. But I do remember being afraid to wet my bed at school. Because if you did, you were afraid someone was going to tell on you. And then someone was going to make fun of you, and you were going to be called a "sissy."

Looking at a muscular, 250-pound tax lawyer, it's sometimes difficult to see the little boy inside who is still afraid of being called a "sissy." But it is healthy to remember the little boy inside. Then, sharing these insecurities, taking them out, examining them, and sometimes learning to laugh about them is the best anecdote to fear.

The "best buddy" myth

So why don't we do more of that with each other? What's wrong? Is it homophobia (a fear of homosexuals, or being thought to be homosexual)? Ever notice how men, when they touch, generally turn it into a slap, punch or bear hug, as long as it's *rough stuff?* "No homo, me!" Or is it the innate competition between men? "If I tell him I'm scared that I'm drinking too much, he's liable to use it against me at work."

Both of these factors play a part, but it's mainly the pre-scribed role of limited acceptable emotional expression imposed upon males practically from the moment of birth. Women per-petuate the problem as well as men, becoming unwitting Code enforcers. Particularly when they make statements such as, "When something serious goes wrong, I look to Brent to take care of it; I see that as part of his role."

And women buy the myth of the male bond. They believe men when they talk about their "close friends" and "best bud-dies."

Don't believe it. Believe the statistics that haunt men like a deathly shadow: more suicides, alcoholism, mental illness, acci-dents. You name it — if it's a bad statistic, men have a corner on the market.

Don't men want to change this? Yes, many do, but it takes a lot of courage and perseverance. They are often ostracized by their fishing buddies if their conversation gets personal, or dropped from their Monday morning quarterback pack if they act de-pressed, preferring to discuss how to deal with mid-life crises rather than whether LSU should have kicked a field goal or gone for the touchdown against Ohio State.

It's easier to find female friends, and they seem better trained for the job. Compassion, tenderness, and empathy are emotions women understand, and sometimes this is what we all, men and women, desperately need.

On a positive note, more and more women I talk to recog-nize the need and the value of male friendships. They worry when they see the men in their lives unable to sustain these friendships. One woman, writing about her husband's lack of male friends at work, even expressed *relief* that he had at least established friendships with women:

Dear Dr. Towery:

My husband has no male friends. I wish he did. There are several women he works with that he talks to regularly, and he really values their advice. Believe me, I'm not jealous — I'd rather him have female friends than no friends at all. I just don't think it's healthy for him to cut men out of his non-work life. Why is he like this?

Most men would like to have closer male friends, but, in general, they find women to be more receptive to their ideas and feelings than other men. While women encourage expression, men feel that other men think less of them for even admitting to their emotions. Other men become uncomfortable, and will often diffuse a friend's attempted openness by indicating to the friend that his behavior is "a little off the wall." It's against the teachings of The Code.

There are ways to overcome the fear of male friendship, such as joining a male support group. Unfortunately, it's usually the guy who is already sensitive who is willing to do this. The men who need it the most wouldn't be caught dead in a support group.

In effect, there is little a wife or loved one can do to help, except be supportive of any good friendship a man forms, realizing that all of us need these human connections. The women he relates to are important, and this particular spouse is wise to be supportive rather than critical of these friendships.

CHAPTER NINETEEN

WHY A FEMALE CONFIDANTE?

Question for women: *If your spouse or partner has close female friends, do you wonder what they share, and importantly, what is the basis for the closeness?*

As a result of unrelenting competition among males, it is not surprising that many turn to female friends for understanding, empathy, and acceptance. Women are simply more comfortable talking about feelings, and examining emotions. Men yearn for communication, but, because of The Code, they deny it to themselves and others.

Even though the role of the female confidante is not a great mystery, it is often interpreted to have sexual overtones. One young reader didn't trust the motivations of a male friend at the office:

Dear Dr. Towery:

For several months now a male manager from another section has come by my office. He is an accountant from 9 to 5, but in his heart, he's a poet. He comes by and shares his work with me. It is very beautiful, and usually reveals very personal feelings. One of my girlfriends says he wants to get me in bed. I don't feel that is the case. He's married with two small children.

Isn't it possible that he just enjoys sharing poetry with a kindred spirit? Or is my girlfriend right — that it has something to do with sex?

While there are no guarantees, the girlfriend is probably wrong. Most men don't have to show women poetry for several months before making sexual advances.

His motivation is probably based on the need to share the poet in himself with another person. It would be more difficult to find a male friend who deeply enjoyed personal poetry. Reading poetry would feel uncomfortable, and would probably fall under the category of "wimpy" for many men.

Why not his wife?

Then the question becomes: Why doesn't he just share this side of himself with his wife? First, she may not like poetry; she may not have an ear for language. Second, many wives feel uncomfortable with "the dreamer" in their spouse. If the wife suspected that her husband wanted to sit in the study and write poetry all day, she might feel nervous about his commitment to the family. After all, how are they going to pay for the trip to Hawaii, the new car, and the kids' private school tuition? Everyone knows "poet" is synonymous with "poor."

So, he plays it safe and finds a female confidante who is not judging him on the basis of whether "he's serious," or a "good provider." A woman who doesn't have *her* dreams hitched to *his* star can marvel at his creativity and spirit, which is the reaction he craves.

Sharing emotions with another woman

The value men place on close, platonic relationships with other women can be a source of frustration for many wives. Many female readers ask me why these relationships exist, or even if they are platonic in nature.

Dear Dr. Towery:

My husband has become close friends with a woman he works with, and they spend a lot more time together than I would like. I get mad about it and lose my temper, accusing them of having sex together. I don't think men and women can get that close and not have sex. Then, he blows up at me and says that I am nuts to suspect such a thing. He says that it is common for men to have women friends they confide in without sex ever entering the picture. Who is right?

To answer her question, specifically, it is common for men to confide in women friends, and sex is usually not part of their relationship. The number one reason is that men generally lack male friends with whom they have established honest, open communication, so they turn to women. It's hard to think of a situation where platonic relationships aren't possible — and probably more likely to occur than love relationships between the sexes.

Many, if not most wives, are aware of the "other woman" in their mate's life. That's the person to whom he confides his dreams, doubts, fears, and fantasies — all of the things the wife wants to hear, but is often not privy to.

A platonic relationship gives a man the chance to talk his feelings out without being judged and given a score ranging somewhere on the success-failure scale. With a platonic female friend he doesn't have to perform; he can just be, like the poet described above.

Interestingly enough, while concern about their husband's fidelity is something many women may worry about, the greatest fear and anxiety seems to be that their husband is sharing the intimacy of his thoughts and feelings with someone else.

Many women can pass a husband's sexual encounter off as just being something physical, but the idea that their husband might share his innermost thoughts with another woman is more than they can take. Real intimacy is what most women crave from their husbands. Instead, wives often find out or suspect that their husbands tell things to other women that they withhold from them. As one woman revealed to me in an interview, "I could care less if she screws his brains out, it saves me the trouble. But if he tells her things he keeps from me, I'll murder him."

Emotional solace

Findings from *The McGill Report on Male Intimacy* sub-stantiate the large number of men who do turn to another woman for emotional solace. Author Michael E. McGill, Ph.D., con-cludes: "The attention given to thoughts of sex and the threat of sex between a man and another woman by all parties — husband, wife and the other woman — tend to overshadow what is most important about these relationships."[50] The significant finding is that an estimated two out of every three men are in some impor-tant way as intimate with other women as they are with their wives.

Of this number, McGill found that half had disclosed infor-mation about themselves to other women that they had not shared with their wives. In fact, reports from both the men and women involved revealed that these were not superficial revelations, but significant self-disclosures.

To understand why this happens, it is important to realize how casual the typical relationships are between men. They build relationships together based on commonality of interests or work. Secondly, it is important to come to terms with the wife's contri-bution, be it ever so subtle.

The story of Herb and Ann

How do you think it feels, for example, when you try to tell your wife about your dream job in the Bahamas and she draws in her breath and grimaces. If Herb (who wants to start a small radio station in the islands with their savings), confides his dreams to his wife, Ann, she may panic and react angrily because her secu-rity is threatened.

In these situations, she doesn't have to scream to get her point across: she's nervous. She is left wondering what she and the children will do if Herb walks away from his paycheck and really invests in his dream. It's her turn now for sweaty palms and night terrors — until he gives it up, which he usually does.

Not to be dismissed is that Ann's perception of Herb changes. He is no longer the stable, secure provider she bargained for when she married him. Suddenly, he is a dreamer, unpredictable, perhaps not someone she can count on for the long haul. It is *his* dream, not *their* dream.

Her feelings may be valid, but that's not the point. Since most men are caught up in their narrow role of provider, is it any wonder that they turn to a third party — often a woman — when it comes time to reveal inner yearnings?

Fortunately, as women's roles change, and they assume a more aggressive position in terms of providing for their families, they won't feel as helpless in these situations. As women continue to expand their roles at work and within the family, men will be given more flexibility. Part of the positive fallout will be the husband's ability to reveal more of the dreamer in himself.

Dear Dr. Towery:

I had a neat experience the other night. I decided to tell my wife that we should invest in a bed and breakfast in New England and forget all the fast track crap. I thought she might get upset if I suggested I wanted to chuck my $55,000 a year job as a comptroller.

I was writing because I hoped you might give other men the message. You see, I've sweated for two and a half years trying to figure out how I could convince my wife that this was a good idea. Sometimes women aren't who we think they are. Maybe another guy can save himself the big sweat.

That's the idea. But it won't happen for everyone right away. I agree, though, that many things you just have to try in order to find the response. And obviously, it's wrong to assume the outcome will be negative.

As more women get burned out on the corporate track themselves or take on more responsibility for paying the bills, they will become less intimidated by the thought of a guy following his dream. It won't be a direct threat to their security, so they can respond to the idea on a more objective basis — as a friend would.

CHAPTER TWENTY

THE NEED FOR REAL
MALE FRIENDSHIP

Question for men: *Do you value the advice and input of a trusted male friend because you feel he's been there — he understands?*

Sometimes nobody can understand a man like another man. We've walked in each other's shoes, felt the same pressures, nurtured the same dreams. Real male friendship, the kind that is often uncomfortable and troublesome, but necessary if there is to be meaning to our lives, is a concept long overdue.

In many ways, men's interactions with other men — whether it be with drinking buddies or business colleagues — is valuable groundwork for the next stage of genuine communication. But it only works if the two men can take it to another dimension. What is frustrating is that they are setting up the basis to communicate, but few rarely pass to the next level.

A verbal shorthand

These men have already established a verbal shorthand, a commonalty of language that is referred to as "male talk." When two men are on the same wavelength, another male's input can be masterfully incisive. The conversations move quickly, the words come easily.

And no matter how much these men may value their female friends, it is different. "I love my women friends," one accountant confides, "but I have to address so many peripheral issues before I get to the meat of the conversation. Sometimes it's frustrating."

The ease of communication comes from a range of experiences that are common to the male gender, all of which fall under the parameters of The Code. A girl of thirteen, for example, can have career dreams, but few women understand the pressure that hits a boy as he enters high school.

"I remember the day my father sat me down, after my bar mitzvah," recalls Hal, a thirty-four-year-old art dealer. "He told me I needed to get serious and chart my course for success. Otherwise, I wouldn't be able to support a family. All I wanted to do was go paint landscapes. I didn't want to think about my financial future."

He's been there

Coupled with these early shared experiences are the ones men encounter as they pursue their careers. One self-made millionaire I know puts it this way: "My male friends are very much like me. They have reached my level of success — but not the easy way. Each of us has had setbacks and cleared major hurdles. We've been on the field of battle together and have won and lost tough contests. They know how it feels to have blood on your face and sand in your eyes."

During a conversation, these men quickly get at a gut-level type of communication. And what they say to each other registers heavily. "When I do get advice from another man, who I think has my best interests at heart, I listen," explains Nick, a young stockbroker. "I'm not sure I can put my finger on it. It's just a feeling of respect for his opinion that I think you can only get with another guy. He's been there. I feel I'm not going to be sidetracked or misled."

It's not elitism, but men simply have a common bond of experience that allows them to cut through the bull with each other. Fortunately, men are beginning to seek out each other's counsel concerning their feelings and fears, just as they have always exchanged opinions on buying cars or stock. The phrase, "He's been there," pinpoints the intrinsic value of male friend-ships.

Other positive aspects of male friendships

A psychiatric nurse I interviewed noted one of the most striking positive aspects of male friendships. In her words: "Men know how to set boundaries and can support each other in a non-instrusive way. Female friendships can become too emotionally invasive."

For example, when her husband was scheduled for prostate surgery, he and his best friend went to a football game together. They never even mentioned his surgery. They discussed the quar-terback and drank beer. "I was appalled at first," she says. "I would have been absolutely maudlin if I were scheduled for any surgery. It turned out all right for him, but I know I would have expected my women friends to get right down in the dumps with me." In retrospect, she realized that these men were coping — it's just that their coping style was different. *They didn't need to talk — they knew.*

"Women almost expect transference with each other," she adds. "We expect another woman to feel everything we're feel-ing, and if she doesn't we're disappointed. My husband doesn't require that from his friends. A nod of the head is sufficient. I think we [women] want blood and guts, and if we don't get it, we don't think we're relating."

This explains why many women are frustrated in their rela-tionships with men. Men, by and large, don't see the virtue in empathy. They set their sites on problem-solving, which leaves many women feeling that "he doesn't understand, he doesn't know, or care, what I'm going through."

One couple I know almost divorced when their teenage son, Jeff, became addicted to drugs. "I started to think my husband didn't care about Jeff at all," she says in relating their story. "The only difference I noticed in him was that he began to throw himself harder into his work. I was torn apart."

After weeks of marriage counseling, the truth emerged: "I thought the best thing I could do was to keep the show on the road, keep on keepin' on," her husband said in one session. I was dying inside, but I had to keep going. The last thing I thought the family needed was for me to crack up. And I've always believed that, 'when the going gets tough, the tough get going.' " Under the rules of The Code, he didn't have any other option.

Men also help each other in terms of goal-setting or in defining limits for their career risks. This goes back to the notion that men value each other's opinions.

An engineer I know was thinking about selling his firm and starting a new venture. "I needed objective advice," he says. "I wanted someone to look at the cold facts." He turned to a male college friend in a different field entirely. Why? As he puts it: "Because he has a way of sorting through the pros and cons like nobody else I know. And he's not afraid to tell me if I've lost my mind."

The same is true for many aspects of a man's life. "If I were going to invest in a mutual fund, I wouldn't call a stockbroker. I'd call my best friend first," the same engineer remarks. "And if I were on my way to Las Vegas, I'd want his opinion on how much money to play with. He cuts through the bullshit, and he isn't emotionally invested like my wife."

Learning to change

As illustrated in the story of Frank, Byron, Trent, and Paul, men are usually fair-weather friends. The friendships exist when things are okay, but they aren't there for the highs and lows. Often they are summarily abandoned when they become trouble.

The friendships are also goal-oriented, often with men approaching the relationships as a stair-stepping event to some type of personal gain or success. At the very least, there has to be a common interest or pursuit in order to "justify" the time spent together. This can include anything from bowling to hunting to drinking together.

Without a common event or pursuit, men ask: "Why else would we spend time together?" The idea of just going to lunch together to catch up — as so many women do — is foreign to men.

In focus groups, for example, I have asked the men how they would feel if another member called them a week later and invited them to lunch. A stockbroker sums up the typical reaction: "I would wonder why we were going to lunch. I would feel more comfortable, in fact, if I knew his agenda. I mean, does this guy want to sell me life insurance, or what?"

Women win hands down in terms of talking just to talk. There is an undeniable virtue in "small talk" that men haven't yet learned. It sets the basis for emotional sharing. As one of my friends puts it, "Maybe it would be hard to move from a discussion of V-6 engines to 'my wife's cheating on me.' But at least it would be a start. I can't do that. When I'm depressed about something, I just keep to myself. I figure my [male] friends don't want to hear about it."

The Code at its best. Hide your pain and your inadequacies at all costs. Don't give the enemy a cheat sheet of your worst fears.

In an effort to hide certain aspects of themselves, men also typically compartmentalize friendships, allowing different friends to see only one part. For instance, Ed may share his enthusiasm for golf with John. He may discuss investments with Phillip. But neither of these two "friends" would have substantial personal knowledge of Ed. It's an issue that perplexes many women. Not long ago, one wife wrote:

Dear Dr. Towery:

Ted and I have lived together for over two years and I like to think I understand him pretty well. But when it comes to his male friends, I obviously don't. Two weeks ago, Joe, his hunting and drinking buddy, was at the house and I asked him what he thought about Ted's promotion at work. He hadn't heard about it! After he left, Ted chewed me out for mentioning anything about his job to Joe.

Last week, we were out to dinner with Larry, his best friend at work, and his date. Larry said how much he liked to duck hunt, and I said that now I know why they get along so well, since Ted does, too. I knew immediately by the way Ted cut his eyes at me I had messed up again. Sure enough, when we got into the car he went into a rage. In both cases he said basically the same thing: that he doesn't want everybody messing in his life and knowing his business. Is this crazy, or am I?

No, the reader isn't crazy. Ted is simply typically male in that he not only compartmentalizes feelings, but also friendships as well. Men seldom talk to one friend about all areas of their lives, as do women. They almost always leave themselves an escape route. While women frequently measure their friendships by the breadth of knowledge of the other, men rarely think in such terms, as Dr. McGill points out in *The McGill Report on Male Intimacy.*[51] Unfortunately, it's a method men use to circumvent real intimacy, and represents an area in which they can learn much from women.

McGill also identifies another great strength of female friendships that is absent in male friendships: "Male relationships are time-bound . . . . Time freezes what men know of one another; it expands what women know of one another."[52]

What he means is that men use time as a limiting definition. A man identifies a friendship as knowing a person during one particular period in a certain context. Women, on the other hand, see friendship as a vehicle to describe the evolution in their lives in all its fullness and complexities.

One female writer I know, for instance, sometimes has lunch with two male editors who worked with each other years ago. "The lunch always centers on their days at the newspaper together. The scoops they pulled off, who was a jerk and who was an okay guy," she observes. "It's as though they've sealed the present and future off. It's downright eerie. They never talk about their present life!"

This is what McGill means by time-bound relationships. Women, by comparison, feel comfortable in using past experiences as a bridge to understanding what their friends are dealing with in the present.

"Melissa was my college roommate," the same writer says in defining her relationship with another woman who now lives over a thousand miles away. "But we rarely talk about school. We talk about her new marriage, my career, or when we plan to have children. In fact, if all she wanted to talk about was our college days, I'd be bored. Maybe even insulted."

Hopefully, men can start learning from women. We men need to view each other as valuable assets to be shared, rather than enemies to be feared. Men need to learn from the feminist movement that no one has a right to tell them what they should be. Once the "shoulds" are dispensed with, friendship and sharing become a much more reasonable alternative to going it alone.

As we have seen, there are definite strengths in male friendships, and these could become even more powerful when integrated with the attributes found in female relationships. Both men and women can learn from each other, integrate the individual strengths, and find a comfortable balance.

CHAPTER TWENTY-ONE

INTIMACY WARS

Question for women: *Do you find yourself wishing that the man in your life was more sensitive? Do you also have difficulty finding a way to his vulnerable side?*

In defining intimacy wars between men and women it might be simpler to say that the battle is really over the insides of a man. It's centered on The Code and how it limits a man's ability to express himself. The perpetual question seems to be: What's going on in there? Anything?

I've met with women who think they know the answer and it isn't a nice one. But the fact is, men have traditionally been rewarded for showing the least amount of emotionalism.

Defining intimacy

Before progressing, it's important to define intimacy. Intimacy between a man and a woman is being close emotionally and physically. Ideally, neither person is afraid of sharing their inner lives — their dreams and secrets — for fear of rejection.

Intimacy also means the ability to give without the fear of being used, believing instead that the other person values what you give and is willing to do the same for you. In a way, intimacy represents an act of faith, faith that the other person will act in your best interests, will stand by your side. If you start thinking that the other person is deliberately doing things to hurt you, something is definitely wrong and you need to talk about it or get help to deal with the issue.

Intimacy is difficult to sustain, but you shouldn't look at it as work. It includes playing and laughing and looking at the other person's shortcomings and your own and saying, "That's okay. We don't have to be perfect today."

A word on differences

Before succumbing to the temptation to say that men just need to let go more, it's important to look at some fundamental differences between the sexes. Differences that won't go away.

Men and women not only speak a different language, we interpret language differently. Men think in spatial terms, women more verbally, more intuitively. The left cortex, or analytical side of the male brain is typically more developed than the right — the opposite of most women. Little girls have stronger verbal skills, and they retain that edge throughout life.

The most recent studies bear this out. For example, differences in the brain structure of male and female rats allow the males to learn to navigate a maze more quickly. But females are less fooled by changes in landmarks, according to researchers Christina Williams, a psychologist at Barnard College, and Warren H. Mech at Columbia University.

Male rats find food in a maze by learning about the geometric proportions. They focus on angles and distances. Female rats store information about geometric shapes but also about landmarks. If the angles and distances are changed, males have difficulty negotiating the maze. Females, by comparison, can rely on the landmarks to help them find their way.

Creative problem solving

All of this doesn't mean that one sex is superior to the other. In a creative problem-solving workshop, focusing on left brain/ right brain differences, for example, the group leader explained that a left brain thinker would take a different approach to assembling a bicycle from scratch than a right brain personality. Typically, the left brain (analytical type) would pull out the instructions and follow every step in order. The right brain type would probably dive into the parts and start fitting them together in a way that made sense to him.

Both people would, in all probability, end up with the same result: an assembled bicycle. Unfortunately, we have a temptation to judge, to say one approach is better than the other. It's important to remember that the results, be it a bicycle, a more cohesive working relationship, or a strong marriage, are what really count.

In male-female relationships, it's far more productive to try and understand the power of The Code than trying to make a man act more like a woman. As choices go, the latter approach isn't going to work!

Men are still caught in an internal conflict, jerry-building their emotions to meet the requirements of the male role: strong and silent. Only certain emotions, such as anger, are patched through to the surface.

What do I mean? How many men, for example, would honestly confess, "I'm lonely." Few. They tend to transpose that feeling into a goal, perhaps telling a friend, "I need to get laid." This is male talk, and unless you recognize it when you hear it, you may fall into the trap of thinking that this guy only cares about a shallow conquest.

Intimacy derailed

Many times couples find themselves pushing the same issues under the carpet again and again. For one reason or another, one or the other begins to feel ignored, invisible:

Dear Dr. Towery:
I feel like an old horse that's been put out to pasture. My husband acts so indifferent to me since I've hit my fifties I don't know what to do.

At first I thought it was menopause. But I didn't feel that different, so why should he change? But he has. Even if I take great care to look my best, he never seems to notice. If we go out to dinner, we have nothing to talk about. Is this just the typical man's reaction to an aging wife?

There are myriad reasons why one partner becomes invisible to the other one. It usually has little to do with looks. There may be something below the surface that hasn't been resolved.

For one, he may think his wife has lost interest and is just responding in kind. He may have pressures on him that he thinks are unfair — pressures he relates to the relationship. One reader shared the following:

Dear Dr. Towery:

Maybe something is wrong with me. A year ago my wife and I moved into her dream home. She loves it. But the mortgage is bigger than I am. Every time I suggest we go "downwardly mobile" she gives me the silent treatment. I'm beginning to hate her. She sleeps like a baby, and I walk the floor wondering how I'm going to make the next payment.

I know other men have gotten themselves into similar jams. What are you supposed to do? I know you won't recommend murder.

The man's very first reference to "her dream home" is a dead giveaway. Anytime a couple chases separate goals they are heading for trouble. It's okay if you understand the risks and make sure one partner isn't getting a raw deal. For the man above, it sounds like he has to put all of his personal goals on hold to keep his wife in "her dream house."

When discussing goals, there has to be a his, hers and us column. Just having a "her" column is asking for trouble, no matter how nice a guy you think you are.

My advice: Put the house up for sale. The financial strain sounds too serious. Nothing is fun when you can't pay the bills.

If the man and woman have a decent relationship, they can work it out and reshape new dreams together. If the woman can't stand it, maybe she doesn't belong in the relationship in the first place.

The fall guy

Our day-to-day discussions often mask our true feelings. We fall into predictable discussions that don't get to the heart of the issues we really need to talk about. The following letter makes the point:

Dear Dr. Towery:

Every time my wife gets mad at me I can be sure of one thing. She's going to mention the fact that our son is in public school and that he should be in private school. I work hard. I'm an attorney in the public defender's office. We have long hours and little reward for what we do. Why can't my wife accept that public schools are okay?

I suspect that the wife isn't all that angry about public schools versus private schools. A promising young lawyer I know decided to devote his career to defending the rights of the mentally ill. A few years into the practice, his wife left him. She said she had bargained for a life of leisure, not watching her husband work tirelessly for so little money, defending people she considered "low-class." In effect, she said he was stupid.

Many of the expectations we bring into a marriage are unrealistic. It's easy for a twenty-year-old to profess undying love under all circumstances. By the time we are in our thirties and forties, however, we realize that love and marriage aren't as easy as we dream.

The commitment differential

Men and women bring different expectations and needs to the table. Men, more so than women, marry for love. Women tend to analyze a potential spouse by many different criteria, including security, social status, and earning power. This introduces the question of why women are more pragmatic and men are more idealistic when it comes to choosing a mate.

While it runs counter to the popular notion of the emotional woman and the practical man, the reason this still happens is tradition. Historically, a woman's only means of support was through her father or her spouse. She had to be practical or she and her children would be out on the street.

Some people chafe at the idea that women are still looking for a wealthy catch. But I still hear it:

Dear Dr. Towery:

I feel like I'm in the 18th century. I teach at a private university well-known for its scholastics. One of the things I dreaded was the competition to excel because I had had enough of competition in grad school.

Boy, did I have a surprise! My fellow women teachers seem to care less about what courses they get or how much they pub-lish. No . . . they compete on the following items: (1) wealth of husband; (2) how pretty or smart their children are; (3) and what contributions they are making to the university.

You can imagine where I'm at? I have no spouse, no chil-dren, and I rent an apartment. How can I put these women in their place? This is ridiculous.

I'm afraid these women are in "their place," and a very uncomfortable one it is. In the face of superficial values, the best thing to do is reaffirm your belief in your own value system. Look for other people who share your ideas. They are there, but it may take some time to find them.

The marital bond

Although there are many women's magazines and books that foster the notion that men are becoming commitment allergic, that is not really true. Married men fare better psychologically than their single counterparts. And once married the majority of men stay married or remarry more quickly than women.

It's time to analyze who is saying, "The male won't commit. The male runs from intimacy." Much of the pop psychology literature is geared to women who are not happy in their current relationships. The unfair, spill over effect is that this literature focuses on a minority of men who do fit the Don Juan mold and don't want to settle down with one woman.

But that denies the existence of the thousands of other men who are sensitive and willing to commit. Most of the young men I interviewed or met at seminars do not take a cavalier attitude towards relationships, and they want very much to have a wife and family.

One of the obstacles, however, is The Code. According to its dictates, a man, to be a real man, must be able to face any and all things alone. This inevitably leads him into a corner where he feels unable to talk about his needs or his vulnerabilities. He *looks* like he doesn't need anyone.

In order to understand the level of the male bond it is important to learn "male talk," or the man's unique way of expressing his emotional needs and caring. For example, instead of saying, "I need you," to a woman, he would say, "I can always count on you."

He might jokingly say to her, "I guess I couldn't shake you off if I tried." What he is really communicating is: "I trust you — I think you'll be there for me."

Or when she walks into a room looking radiant, he may laugh and say, "no flies on you tonight." Which means, "You are beautiful."

Unfortunately, women tend to wait for words or expressions that many men will never say, except in syrupy Harlequin novels or soap operas. In these examples, the hero takes a deep breath and says to the fragile, exquisite heroine, "There has never been a woman as beautiful as you. I will love you till the end of time.

If anyone ever tries to harm you, I will kill them with my bare hands."

You can hear the violins coming up in the background. Of course, real men feel sick at the thought of saying such things. It's like asking a horse to run backwards. It isn't going to work. The horse isn't built that way.

Speaking the same language

Although the language of love may be different for men and women, giving and sharing sexual pleasure is remarkably simple. Oh, we try to make it complicated. There's The Code's prevailing notion that men should be ever-ready, gymnastic studs, and women should swoon from earthshaking orgasms.

Great sex happens when two people are in love and trust each other. They relax and forget who is giving and who is receiving pleasure. It melds into one. It has little to do with who has the most wondrous orgasms. But we tend to second-guess ourselves in this arena more so than any other, as the following letter shows:

Dear Dr. Towery:

I am fairly young and Matt is the second guy I've been to bed with. I love him very much, but he has me worried. He always says we have great sex and I don't know what that means. Does that mean that's all we have? What are men talking about when they say that? Am I going to let him down if I don't have an orgasm?

As a general rule, two people don't have great sex unless they have a good relationship going into the bedroom. The bedroom can't patch up a bad relationship, and it can't be the only place two people enjoy each other.

One of the greatest gifts you can give a partner is your honest response — not what you think they're looking for. If you start worrying about letting someone down, you increase the chances for doing just that.

Sexual pleasure isn't something that should be closely orchestrated. It should be freely shared and allowed to develop its own rhythm. Sometimes we're in the mood for closeness, for hugging and holding hands. Sometimes it's more tempting, for both men and women, to enjoy a passionate "quickie." Sometimes we just want to sustain the moment and go as slowly as we can. And all of that is okay.

The only rule is that there shouldn't be a scorecard on the headboard.

CHAPTER TWENTY-TWO

THE CODE'S DEADLY EQUATION: PERFORMANCE FOR LOVABILITY

Question for women: Have you ever noticed how one failure in the sexual arena can leave a man devastated, and worse yet, unable to talk about it?

Women today are more willing to discuss sexuality. Many therapists will tell you that female patients spend more time talking about sex than men. And they aren't afraid to share specific details.

Men, by and large, don't like discussing sex. If that sounds crazy, let's define our terms. Oh, men love *bragging* about sex. *Lying* about sex is another popular one. *Joking* about sex is an area where men win hands down. But *discussing* sex? No way. It's unmanly and embarrassing. And the sex they do talk about is always oblique, through jokes or hazy references to others — never specifically about themselves or someone they have feelings for.

The compulsion to perform

Men must always be ready, willing, and able to have sex, or something is dead wrong. Doesn't everyone know that all men are just slaves to their macho sex drives, and if one's sex drive is not in high gear for a period of time, then what's wrong with him?

Additionally, the poor guy is probably going to withhold telling anyone that he has any problems or doubts when it comes to the bedroom. While 75 percent of the letters I receive from my readers are from women, I can pull in hundreds of letters from men any time I want to by writing about one subject: sexual dysfunction in general, or impotence in particular. If I tell them I will send them a free brochure on impotency, the post office can't handle the mail. They will always send a self-addressed envelope, so the secretary won't open the letter and discover their "weakness."

As The Code becomes ingrained in a man's psyche, he begins to see all actions he performs in win/lose terms. This is played out with tragic vengeance in the bedroom, where the male feels he must always be better — better than the woman, better than any lover she's had in the past, better than whatever fantasies she may have about a sexual partner now. That's a tough order to fill night after night, especially as he tires from the stress of work and age.

Equating lovability with performance

Equating lovability with performance is debilitating to true intimacy. Yet, men, indoctrinated under The Code, continue to measure their ability to please and be worthy of love based on their performances. That is as true in the bedroom as it is in the world of business or the sports arena.

Women who try to establish intimacy with these men become frustrated. The women seem to hit a brick wall — a wall constructed over a number of years and often impenetrable.

Whose fault is it?

Many self-help and pop psychology books tell you that it's probably the man's fault. When sexual intimacy is not satisfying for a couple, one of the more common reactions is to level blame. Counterproductive guilt and shame follow. Sadly, women blame themselves while the male tends to pull into his shell.

One of the worst mistakes is to try to establish "whose fault this is." In all probability, the male is doing his best to match the definition of manhood that he learned from locker room talk, while the female is making heroic efforts to make him more like a "new man" — more sensitive, more understanding, easier on himself and others.

But men and women have different concerns and different needs for intimacy. This certainly holds true for sex. And it simply doesn't work to try and say the differences don't exist.

The beat goes on

One of the best descriptions of the different approaches of men and women to sex is found in the rhythms of music. As Maggie Haselwerdt writes in *Rock & Roll Confidential:*

The beat of rock 'n' roll may be the beat of sexual intercourse, but for the most part, it's intercourse from the male point of view. Though female sexuality is one of the stronger flavors in musical brew when it comes to blues, soul, and dance music, rock's driving beat, piercing guitar lines, pounding keyboards, and expansive, stage-dominating gestures marks the territory as male.

Female sexual response, which in case you don't know I will tell you, is slow-building rather than focused, buzzing rather than pouncing, melting rather than hardening, and cyclical rather than constant. And it's not often reflected or catered to in rock.

. . . the best song is "Be My Baby," which owes its uncanny power to wholesale appropriation of female patterns of sexual response. Phil Spector and the Ronettes weave a gauzy curtain around the sexual impulse, diffusing and romanticizing it, blurring the focus with walls of vibrating sound, highlighting the drama of the encounter with a series of minute yet heart-stopping pauses. . . .[53]

The scorecard mentality

The Code eventually leads to a scorecard mentality, where the man is constantly measuring himself and feeling measured. If you think the pressure a guy feels on a football field with girls watching is intense, wait until he gets into bed! Throwing a football is one thing, but to risk one's very manhood on whether or not an organ, over which the man has no conscious control, gets erect — that's high risk.

If he allows it, a man can let The Code cripple his ability to enjoy intimacy without feeling that his actions — his erections, etc. — are always being gauged. Worse yet, if he listens to the guys in the locker room or watches TV or goes to see movies — if he's a normal guy — he probably has an overrated view of how other men perform, and he starts feeling that he never measures up.

If a woman really wants to damage her partner, and ultimately her relationship with him, all she has to do is compare him unfavorably to other lovers. And all it takes is one single time. The following letter is a case in point:

Dear Dr. Towery:

Mindy and I have been together for five years. We usually get along very well. However, lately when we do have serious arguments she does something that demolishes me and is beginning to make me feel it's time to get out.

When she gets really mad at me, she says I can't perform sexually like her last boyfriend could. Not as often, not as long, not as well. We have a lot invested in our life together, but I don't know how long I can endure this humiliation.

This man has endured it longer than most might. By humiliating him, does his partner really think that now when they go to bed he is going to be relaxed and fun? He's going to be as scared as a boy on his first date.

No matter how great she may be most of the time, there is never a reason for denigrating another person's sexual capacity. For many of us, men and women, it strikes too close to an already fragile self-concept. The comparisons she makes are intentionally castrating and could lead to sexual dysfunction.

For whatever reason, remarks such as Mindy's reveal that the woman is harboring a great deal of anger and hostility. When there is a lot invested in the relationship and a lot of good times, joint counseling should be considered an option. There are avenues for diffusing anger that don't involve destroying a partner's self-esteem.

Whose fault is it?

One of the worst mistakes we can make is trying to establish "whose fault this is." In all probability, the male is doing his best to follow the definition of manhood he learned as a boy, while the female is making heroic efforts to make him an Alan Alda clone — more sensitive, more understanding, easier on himself and others.

When there is a sexual concern, the male generally feels he has failed — even if he never verbalizes it. In one letter I received that was marked PERSONAL AND CONFIDENTIAL, a benefits manager in his late thirties confided:

Dear Dr. Towery:

I'm afraid that something is wrong with me. I just don't have the interest in sex that I've had before. It's just not there. It's really weird. I feel like I should want something that I really don't care about lately.

I'm closing in on forty so I wonder if this could be the problem I've heard so much about men reaching their peak at eighteen and then downhill from there, and now I think I know why people say that. It really feels true. Should I see a doctor?

Of course, it's never a bad idea to see a doctor in order to rule out a medical cause. Contrary to popular myth, roughly 50 percent of impotence has a physiological basis, according to William L. Furlow, M.D., a urologist and international expert in the diagnosis and treatment of impotence. Dr. Furlow is co-founder of the Center for Urological Treatment and Research in Nashville, Tennessee.

Who has time?

But other factors may be playing a part. Stress, particularly work stress, is the most frequent culprit when it comes to lack of interest in sex. If you think the increasing pressures of today's working couples are blown out of proportion, think again. Research reported in *American Sociological Review* showed a striking decline in the amount of time a dual-career couple spends together.[54]

The average two-income couple only spends 3.2 waking hours together. That's the good news. Wives report that two-paycheck couples spend only 33 minutes a day eating meals together. This doesn't even compare favorably with the time spent by single-earner couples, which is 41 minutes a day.

While the husbands and wives in single-earner couples claim they talk to each other 19 minutes a day, dual earners say they talk to each other about 12 minutes a day. The wives in dual-earner couples also report having fun with their spouses an average of only 28 minutes a day.

Other culprits

There are also numerous body stresses such as drinking and smoking. Both of these adversely affect a male's sexual functioning. The arteries responsible for an erection are damaged by smoking, while alcohol can kill the nerves that signal these vessels to dilate. Evidence shows that the more a man smokes, the greater the damage he sustains. The damage to drinkers, while not necessarily apparent in light to moderate drinkers, is observed regularly in alcoholics.

Problems of sexual desire may also be the culprit — which doesn't mean that either you or your spouse is doing something wrong. In our fast-paced society, lack of desire is affecting more and more adults. Insufficient Sexual Desire (ISD) is the number one sexual dysfunction in America. As many as one in five American adults may be afflicted, according to Dr. Joseph Mendels, medical director of the Philadelphia Medical Institutes and professor of pharmacology and psychiatry, Thomas Jefferson School of Medicine.[55]

According to Dr. Mendels, lay people tend to think of sexual desire as a largely physical process involving interplay between hormone levels, blood flow, and the genitals. Until about four years ago, sex researchers tended to agree. However, scientists now know that desire is mediated primarily by the more primitive areas of the brain — those areas not directly involved in conscious thinking.

Ordinarily, levels of neurotransmitters within the brain keep desire within what we call the "normal ranges." But when these levels become out of balance, the result may be partial or complete loss of sexual interest.

Typically, people suffering from low sexual desire are otherwise healthy. Their hormonal levels are within normal ranges. But the neurotransmitters responsible for switching sexual impulses on and off in the brain may be out of balance. Research is currently underway to investigate a handful of drugs that might possibly restore the balance.

But before hoping for a medical cure, doctors are quick to point out that sexual-desire problems may have a simple explanation. Many medications may inhibit the sex drive, including high blood-pressure medications, antidepressants, and ulcer medications.

Another possibility for lack of interest in sex is anger. Men have a particularly difficult time identifying and dealing with slow-burning anger or resentment toward their partners. And they often don't understand when it manifests itself in bed. They may hold back something they know would please their partner without realizing that repressed anger is the cause.

If this is a possibility, it's time to sit down and think out what grudges or resentments you have toward your partner. It's kind of hard to be intimate and loving and great in bed — for these are the qualities that almost all women confide make great lovers — if you secretly want to wring your partner's neck.

An honest evaluation of your relationship and your feelings toward your partner should help you to see whether resentments have been slowly building up and need to be resolved. One of the simplest ways to air things out is to make a list of what is working in your relationship and what is not. Find out what resentments each of you harbor — but do it in the spirit of an investigation, not a hanging.

For example, the wife might think financial matters are working, but the husband might think he is being backed into a corner. She needs to know that. Conversely, she may think the sex is great. He may not realize that she really does feel that way. So, unearth the good with the bad, and then tackle the problem areas separately. It may have taken you months or years to become strangers, so don't try to rush through a quick fix.

The body clock

There is always the possibility that your body is slowing down somewhat, and your sexual needs are indeed dropping. But age as a source of sexual problems is overrated. If all men reach their sexual peak early, then why do many women talk about the joys of older lovers who are more gentle and experienced?

The fact is, when someone mentions the sexual peak at eighteen years of age or so, they're talking about mechanics; how many erections a night a male can muster. Undoubtedly at eighteen he can get more than he can at forty. But as we've seen in this book and countless others written by women, mechanics aren't what women are interested in.

Does a man reach his gentleness peak at eighteen? Does his knowledge of women peak at eighteen? Does his sensitive attitude based on experience peak at eighteen? Nope. He's just getting started. Because a man may no longer want sex every night doesn't mean his sex drive or the relationship itself is going down the tubes. In the best sense, both are maturing.

Too often, we try to compare our sex lives with others in order to establish if we are having the normal amount. Again, sexual mechanics are much easier to measure than our loving sensibilities.

There is no such thing as the "normal" amount of sex. In Woody Allen's *Annie Hall,* Diane Keaton and Woody Allen are both visiting their respective psychotherapists. Each is asked how often they have sex. Diane Keaton says, "God, all the time — about three times a week." Woody Allen says, "Almost never — about three times a week."

Now if you think that means the normal amount is three times a week, you're wrong. The answer is there is no answer. A couple that likes to have sex every two months is as normal as a couple that indulges twice a week. The important point is that both partners agree on how much — and it shouldn't be based on what one or the other thinks "everybody else" is doing.

Sometimes the differences must be addressed, as the following letter indicates:

Dear Dr. Towery:

You've heard this one before. So have I. But this time it's not so funny, since it's happening to me. My husband is a great guy, who says, on those rare occasions he will talk about such things, that he doesn't always like to be the sexual aggressor. That's OK, since we're talking about a liberated woman here.

So, I put on my fluffy high heels, pink teddy, my most compliant personality and meet him at the door with a double martini

(extra dry). He takes the martini, wolfs it down, moans about his
job and heads for the back yard to romp with the dog.

This scene, or something similar, has played at our house
once too often. Sure it's different when we go away, but you can't
take a vacation every time you want sex.

No, you can't always go on vacation. But you can let the guy
get his breath before the Showdown at Sundown. Most businessmen, and businesswomen for that matter, have been working on
somebody else's schedule all day long and are now ready to
follow their own timetable for awhile. People need time to shift
gears.

As for the dog, dogs seldom demand anything from us but
our love, so they usually get it. It's nice to be able to romp and
not feel like someone is going to hold up scorecards when you're
done.

But do you think this woman's husband can talk about this
to his friends? Can you see him at a bar with a bunch of guys
watching a game and saying, "Man, my wife just wants to have
sex all the time! And I just don't feel like being intimate after a
hard day. . . ." In fact, just using words like "intimate," "nurture"
and "feelings" is enough to label a male a wimp.

Unless he's an extremely open guy with unusually open
friends, you won't catch him dead saying such things. His friends
will laugh and say, "What're you, queer? Give me a nympho like
that and I'll go to my grave trying to wear her ass out. I'd love
it!" He doesn't know if they're lying or not. In fact, they don't
know either. But they are.

There's only one solution for resolving "timing" differences
and that's talking. If you're married to a psychic, then you can
disregard this advice, but the rest of us need to pay heed. Your
partner doesn't know what's on your mind unless you tell him or
her. Don't wait for heat to build up and then start launching the
accusations. One male defendant in a divorce proceeding found
out seven years too late that his wife hated sex in the morning.
She never told him; she waited and told the judge.

You should always try to keep the tone of such conversations lighthearted. There's nothing worse than hearing the funeral march in the background when you are trying to work out a sexual difference. Humor can smooth over a number of rough spots, including highly personal preferences regarding sex. After all, sex is supposed to be fun.

You may also find it helpful to read books on sexuality. There are a number of excellent books that focus on understanding human sexuality in technical terms. For instance, you can find an explanation of why a man has difficulty with premature ejaculation — and what can be done to help. One of the best in-depth advice books in this category is *Male Sexuality*.

Towards a resolution

A man going to an Alcoholics Anonymous meeting is not thought of as selfish. Nor is a man who wants to stop smoking. When people seek help for an addiction, they are concerned with themselves and rightfully so. It's the only way they can conquer their problems.

Men are addicted to The Code. A junkie never admits he's a junkie and men won't sit up, unprovoked and say, "Hey — I'm addicted to behaving in a lot of stupid, destructive ways!"

One partner can't walk in with the idea that she is going to "fix" the other person. But she can be a catalyst for change. The other person has to see the benefit, the payoff for him, before he will see the need to set a goal and work toward it.

However, men are usually stubborn about admitting a problem. It's in The Code. Many men enter treatment for impotency only at the prompting of a loving partner. To encourage a loved one to seek help is positive.

There's a fine line we're walking here, but it can be walked. Begin by letting your partner know how much you love and value him. Establish a safety net, so that he or she knows that your love and concern don't depend on performance.

And don't forget to bring along your humor. Don't couch a problem in terms of life and death seriousness. And don't feel you have failed if your partner doesn't respond immediately. Therapists would all go out of business if they could bring about lasting change overnight.

Any change should be rewarded. For the wife who complains that her husband is only affectionate when he wants sex, remember that this is the conditioning he received from childhood. To change this behavior is an important hurdle for the man. He's had a long time to learn The Code. Give him a little time and a lot of help to trash it.

CHAPTER TWENTY-THREE

SEX AND WRINKLES

Question for men: *Do you think your female partner thinks you*
place more emphasis on her aging than you
in fact do?

There seems to be a conspiracy afoot to make women worry obsessively about aging. Many women point to age as the major point where men are given an unfair advantage. Men, they argue, begin to look dignified. In fact the "middle- aged, ruggedly handsome" man is a well-established stereotype in Hollywood. And sure enough, he doesn't have a "ruggedly handsome" counterpart in the movies — or the books. No. She is typically young, fresh, with skin as smooth as silk.

Worse yet, many women assume that age is their sexual enemy. Once they pass an arbitrary line — and start looking old — it's all over for them sexually.

"The dry spells have certainly been longer and more frequent since I was in my twenties," says one woman. "That's just the way it is for a woman who is single and over thirty-five." The author of the words is Susan Jacoby, a free-lance writer who frequently contributes to women's magazines.[56]

"Sex and love are both harder to come by than they were in the days when I could reasonably look upon any man between twenty and eighty as a prospect," she continues, "and when so many of those men were automatically attracted by my youthful face and figure."[57]

More recently, the leading cover line of *Cosmopolitan* magazine read: "How to Look Younger *Longer* and Stop the Clock."[58]

In other magazines, the list continues with teasers such as, "Stay Firmer Longer," "Forty But Fabulous," or "How to Make Love Forever with Your Man."

The idea that a woman's attractiveness ends at a certain age brings to mind one of my favorite quotes: "Let him go where he will, he can find only so much beauty or worth as he carries." The author was American writer Ralph Waldo Emerson. If a woman assumes her self-worth is measured by inches and wrinkles, then old age will knock the wind out of her sails.

And if she carries the idea that her beauty diminishes with each passing year, the light will leave her smile, the shine will leave her eyes. It doesn't take a genius to realize that if you *feel* unattractive, then other people will perceive you as unattractive.

Society's courtship with youth

Women, it seems, are having a difficult time convincing themselves that it is all right to age. In fact, women perpetuate our society's courtship with youth and beauty more so than men. A quick check of women's publications shows that models are typically in their teens or early twenties and wrinkle- and sag-free.

The magazine, *New Woman*, advertises that: "A New Woman Is an Attitude, not an Age." Ironically, the cover of a recent issue lists two of its most important articles as: "Take 5 Years (At Least) Off Your Face," and "Our Hip & Thigh Diet (Exercises, Too)."[59]

Similarly, a recent television commercial for Oil of Olay moisturizer features a beautiful woman saying, "Me, age gracefully? I intend to fight it every step of the way." Commercials such as this continue to give women mixed messages. On the one hand, it's okay to turn forty. But on the other hand, your skin better look more like twenty.

Robin Lichtenstein, the health and lifestyles writer for *The Trenton Times*, in New Jersey, remembers her grandmother being upset by her growing number of wrinkles. "I think there is a beauty in old faces that we don't recognize or value," the writer says. "I used to tell my grandmother that, 'wrinkles are like medals — they mean you have lived, you have seen a great deal of life, that you have endured'."

In her position with the newspaper, Lichtenstein sees numerous press releases on health issues, including the latest studies and treatments for aging. She estimates that 90 percent of the anti-aging products are targeted for women. "Almost all of the material we receive on plastic and reconstructive surgery, for example, is also targeted to women, with the exception of hair transplant treatments," she says.

Women as critics

During one of my seminars, one female manager suggested that it is society that says it is okay for men to have gray hair and wrinkles — but not for women. For support, she pointed to the numerous distinguished older gentlemen who work as TV news anchors. While there are female anchors, they are typically younger and exceptionally beautiful, she argued.

But anchors retain their position based on rating points. Female viewers make those decisions as surely as do male viewers. Our society includes more females than males. There are roughly 119 million males in the country compared to nearly 125 million females, according to the most recent statistics from the United States Department of Commerce Bureau of the Census. Whether it's the Nielsen or Arbitron rating system, a point is a point — they don't weigh the male vote more heavily. Women have at least an equal hand in saying, "We don't want older female anchors."

When it comes to aging, women are far more critical of themselves than they might realize. At a recent conference the name of Barbara Walters came up. The woman next to me suddenly announced: "I don't know why that old bag is still interviewing people. She ought to give the next generation a chance."

It was a cruel statement, made more incomprehensible because this woman was clearly over fifty! Where are women going to find the support to accept the aging process if not among themselves?

The younger woman syndrome

When you introduce the topic of aging in a mixed group, one woman will typically stand up and say, "You *know* men prefer younger women — why not admit it? That's the crux of the problem."

Admittedly, many men are attracted to younger women. But it has far less to do with firm flesh than many women realize. Initially, the attraction may stem from the younger woman's response to an older man's success or status.

A man governed by The Code is particularly susceptible to the charms of a younger woman because she is easier to be with: She is not as likely to press the man for intimate dialogue or badger him into confronting issues he finds painful. In sum, she demands less emotionally from him, and she is usually easier to impress with fewer worldly accomplishments. Specifically, she requires less disclosure, which allows him the power of remaining a mystery.

In any given male-female relationship, two central issues must be resolved: (1) the level of intimacy that both the man and the woman wish to attain; and (2) the issue of power, or who is going to control the pace and intensity of the relationship.

In general, these two issues are simpler to resolve when an older man becomes involved with a younger woman. First of all, younger women tend to accept a much lower level of emotional intimacy than older women. For instance, women who have not yet reached thirty don't ask as many questions. They don't pry. The net effect is that they make it much easier for the man to remain an enigma — something which he feels comfortable with because of The Code.

They also allow the male to set the pace and intensity of the relationship. He never feels out of control. By comparison, an older woman becomes much more adept at ferreting out information, or at knowing what a man is thinking. If he is locked into The Code, the older woman represents a threat. She will see his weak points. She may even comment on them.

By the same token, men who have broken out of some of the limitations of The Code do want to reach for a greater level of intimacy. They are attracted to older women because they can appreciate the wisdom of her years, even her ability to see the whole of him — and still be willing to love and accept him.

Power issues remain tougher. It is more comfortable for both men and women, when the man is viewed as the more powerful partner. As a wealthy female real estate broker once wrote to me:

Dear Dr. Towery:

I am dating a man who is 12 years younger than me. We love each other, but I am currently supporting us. He has graduated from college and is very smart. But he hasn't established himself yet in any business.

That's okay, but when we are at social gatherings, everyone seems to ask him what he does. It's uncomfortable for him, I know. But it's also uncomfortable for me, because inevitably there is a smirk or look of disdain when they realize he isn't "doing something important." I'm sure they also wonder why he isn't with a younger woman — "someone his own age."

I don't know how much longer I can stand it. Will other people ever change? Why does the man always have to be older and better in business than the woman?

The answer begins with these two people accepting what is happening between them. They are breaking an unwritten social contract, and other people are going to apply pressure — if they allow them to do so. It is uncomfortable to take an unpopular position, be it in politics, at the office, or in our personal relationships.

The first step is to acknowledge that it won't be easy and that other people are, in one way or another, going to call attention to it. As my own father used to say, "Don't expect a pat on the back for being different. That's not the way society operates."

Second, it requires believing strongly enough in yourself and your convictions to stand by them. It is also helpful to look at your friends and acquaintances and realize that you probably don't approve of all of their decisions. But that doesn't mean you don't care about them, don't enjoy their company, or won't be there for them.

Unfortunately, when it comes to ourselves, we tend to judge more harshly and want everyone to accept everything we do — maybe even applaud us. And that is unrealistic.

Being true to yourself

In acknowledging the reasons that men are attracted to younger women, it doesn't mean older women should act more like little girls. It does mean that older women should practice self-acceptance. For single women in the forty and above group, lack of self-acceptance is perhaps the biggest stumbling block to forming relationships.

One young woman, writing about her mother, put it well:

Dear Dr. Towery:

I am worried about my Mom. She is only sixty-four years old, but she acts like her life is over. Dad died about three years ago, and my Mom seems to think that "there will never be another man" for her.

I can understand to a point. They were married for forty years. But I know she is lonely. She won't admit it, even if you try to pin her down. Maybe she couldn't find another partner, but she won't even try. Is there something I can say that would make her think young again?

The need for intimacy does not end at any age. But an individual's adjustment to the death of a spouse depends on a variety of factors. These include the person's basic personality,

the quality of their marriage, their current health, and their out-
look on life.

Some widows or widowers cannot trust that another human
being can meet their needs in ways that their former spouse did.
They are correct. And whether or not they would be happy having
their needs met in new ways is a highly personal decision.

If you try to talk someone into a relationship, it is possible
to prove that marrieds are healthier than singles. According to the
National Health Interview Survey (NHIS), published in 1987,
married men and women report the fewest sick days. The survey
sampled more than 47,000 households, containing nearly 123,000
people.[60]

The differences in health and accident risk also increase
with age. Single people aged 18 to 24, for example, are just
slightly more likely to suffer from chronic disabilities than their
married counterparts of the same age. However, one-third of
unmarried men and women aged 45 to 64 are limited in their
activities because of chronic disabilities. Only one-fifth of married men and women in the same age group are limited.

Pushing sexuality into the corner

Many widows and widowers prefer to maintain companionship with friends of the opposite sex. That is perfectly normal. But
it's important for them to be honest about their reasons. If their
failure to reach out sexually is based on lack of self-esteem, that
is another issue.

Unfortunately, society tends to trivialize the sexual needs of
the elderly. We hear sexually active men referred to as "dirty old
men." Similarly, women are called "horny old bags." These are
cruel stereotypes that continue to haunt the elderly and make it
hard for them to maintain dignity in a sexual relationship. Often,
it's their children who give off these messages when they discover that "Pop has a girlfriend."

Self-acceptance

In a society that has gone mad with self-improvement programs it is difficult to learn self-acceptance. We are constantly bombarded with new programs to help us lose weight, expand our consciousness, or learn how to make our wardrobes work. Women are particularly vulnerable to the messages presented in the advertising campaigns for these programs. They are attracted to the promises of "youth restored" or "the easiest weight loss program ever" because they are more self-conscious of their heavy hips or wrinkles than men. But is all this change necessary?

There's an interesting new philosophy about changing our appearances. Many psychologists are beginning to argue that people are better off changing their attitude about their appearance rather than changing their looks. If you know you will feel much better after dropping ten pounds, go ahead. But, if you think a facelift will bring the partner of your dreams into your life, then you are headed for trouble. What is really important is how people feel about their looks. It is far more important than how they actually look.

Women fight flaws harder

Again, women have more difficulty accepting their appearance than men. In Detroit, a recent University of Michigan study of dieting habits found that 38 percent of the girls in grades six through twelve and 49 percent of their mothers considered themselves overweight. In reality, only 15 percent of both groups weighed more than recommended.

The inability to accept your looks is not just a matter of vanity. Both men and women who perceive themselves as physically unattractive tend to suffer from low self-esteem, feel more awkward in social situations, report more sexual problems, and are hit harder by depression.

Codependence

Unfortunately, many people think they can get around feelings of low self-esteem by putting other people's needs before their own. These people, called "codependents," try to feel good about themselves by focusing on the needs of others in their families and in the work place. However, since they haven't developed the skills to meet their own needs, they usually end up frustrated and depressed.

Codependence seems to have reached epic proportions if you listen to the number of psychologists, psychiatrists, and addiction specialists who are treating this behavior disorder. Treatment centers around the country are developing programs for the express purpose of treating codependence.

Simply put, codependents are people who look for their self-esteem in someone or something outside of themselves. It is a learned behavior that stems from the belief that they are somehow defective and at fault. This belief forms when a child grows up in a dysfunctional environment or a family that does not deal with issues directly.

The classic example is a home in which one or both of the parents are practicing alcoholics. The children get caught up in their parents' web of denial. Daddy may have been in a car wreck, but Mom is standing there saying, "don't worry, everything is okay." Yet, the children know everything isn't all right. They have to deal with Mom's denial of what is really going on.

After repeatedly watching a parent do embarrassing or frightening things, the children begin to internalize a sense of shame. They begin to think: "If I were good, I wouldn't be part of a family like this." The environment is out of control. They don't know if Mom can cook dinner because she might have passed out during the soap operas earlier in the afternoon.

In order to survive, the children begin to diminish their emotional, even their physical needs. A woman in a seminar recalled the following example:

When I was eight years old, Daddy promised me a pony for my birthday. Every time he got drunk he said he was going to buy a beautiful pony for his pretty little girl. My birthday came and he came home drunk. My Mom was throwing a party for me and I remember everyone leaving — all the other mothers and the kids. I didn't get a pony. That was my last birthday party, too. My Mom was too embarrassed to invite anyone over. I learned to expect nothing for my birthday. It seemed normal after awhile.

But the emotional deprivation eventually snowballs. And by their late twenties, early thirties, children from an environment like this end up hurting inside. Often their personal relationships don't work out well. They never learned to express needs clearly, and no partner can be a mind reader.

They often don't acknowledge their needs — even to themselves. The woman above went from one low-paying secretarial job to the next even though she had a master's degree in art history. She didn't value herself, so she didn't expect anyone else to either. Only after working with a therapist for six months did she begin to see the self-destructive patterns she had developed.

The bottom wrinkle

The bottom line is, if you aren't being a friend to yourself, you need to start working on that relationship. If you recognize that this relationship isn't what it should be, go ahead and shift the focus to yourself for awhile. Tell your partner, your friends, and family.

In order to bolster self-esteem, it helps to find something you can master, whether it is gardening, writing poetry, cooking omelettes, or swimming laps. Through simple activities you can develop a greater awareness of your physical and emotional needs.

All of these come into focus during moments of self-acceptance, during those moments we "selfishly" set aside to do our thing. These times can simply be moments when you sit or lie down and relax.

While other people can meet many of your deepest needs, the happiest people are those who don't indulge in magical thinking — the notion that someone else will wave a wand and make it all better for them. By being your own best friend, you can be your own best source of wisdom. Ultimately, you will reap the rewards of having more to share with those around you.

How it changes her

Many women become more attractive as they grow older. They mature in different ways, including their sense of style, their demeanor, their self-confidence.

Going back for a high school or college reunion after twenty years bears this out. Men often report that the most attractive women are often the ones that looked "a little mousey back in school." It happens so often that it's really become a cliché — where the so-so girl next door blossoms into a beautiful, vibrant women in her thirties and forties.

When hearing from men across the country, whether in letters or interviews, I noticed an interesting pattern. Men, as a rule, are concerned about their partner's aging in direct relation to how much it changes her — and their relationship. In other words, if the woman suddenly loses interest in their shared hobbies, or all interest in sex, then her aging becomes a relationship issue.

Most men are attracted to women of all ages who retain their spirit and interest in life. These are women who are in touch with the little girl inside themselves. It is the responsibility of the woman to be in touch with the little girl, and the same is true for men being in touch with the little boy inside. In the best relationships, the two children learn how to be playful together and stay playful.

The wisdom and patience of age

Often, men stop noticing the women with whom they are in love. Many married men report heated arguments when they fail to notice if their spouse has changed her hair or bought a new dress. A man will say, "You look pretty tonight," and the woman will ask what he *specifically* thinks is so pretty about her tonight. Women are often on to the fact that men will try to get off easy with a generalization that doesn't require real effort. Men are mystified at this behavior.

But what becomes more important as a relationship matures are shared values — be they spiritual values, a similar approach to finances, or child rearing.

Are men better able to handle a partner's aging than women give them credit? A qualified "Yes." Men confirm that it is important that their spouses want to stay healthy and in shape.

But it doesn't take a Rhodes Scholar to realize that women are going to age. What becomes more important to a mature man are personal qualities, such as tactful deliveries of insights, or sharing the feeling that both partners are watching out for each other.

In her book *Perfect Women,* Colette Dowling captures the all-too-typical focus of women on their outer selves. In fact she could be addressing codependence:

> *This essentially is what all females do. It is from our image in the mirror and our reflection in the eyes of others that we try to derive a sense of security, some grounds for self-esteem. Out of touch with our inner selves, we rely excessively on our outer selves. We can change our outer selves, "improve" our outer selves, and thus secure the attention we so desperately require. "Body Narcissism," psychiatrists call it. Our faces, our bodies, our hair become excessively important. The woman who has always been told she has beautiful hair comes to rely on her hair for her very definition of herself.*[61]

Women are beginning to move beyond the constraints of defining self through their reflection in others. Dowling herself shows much personal courage throughout her book in exposing the fallacies of codependence and offers much hope.

As women grow more connected to the gifts of age, including its wisdom and patience, so can the men in their lives. As a mature man grows in love with his partner, he can see a different level of beauty. He can appreciate her caring and vulnerable side more. Is it important? Yes. But it is only one aspect of the relationship, only one spoke in the wheel.

Men repeatedly say they care less about the sags and wrinkles on women than women do. It's important to note the qualification these men are issuing: "We care less about wrinkles than women do."

The point is, women continue to care a lot. In spite of the aging of the Baby Boomers, we have not graciously come to terms with the effects of aging. We are still a wrinkle-phobic society. That won't change overnight.

It's impossible to destroy the American fascination with youth and beauty. It's a phenomenon that's as strong as The Code. But it doesn't have to be the central theme of life. It's possible to look at it, hopefully laugh at it, learn to live with it — and move on to more important themes.

CHAPTER TWENTY-FOUR

THE OLD MAN AND THE CODE

*Question for women: Are you aware that your partner is prob-
ably more sensitive to his own signs of
aging than yours?*

If you take a group of people and mention the male mid-life
crisis, the women tend to smile knowingly and nod their heads.
The men become uncomfortable and look around as if they don't
know what you're talking about.

One explanation of this dual response is that women are
conditioned culturally to accept that they go through phases. They
are accustomed to being accused of being in the middle of PMS,
going through the change, having the vapors or just changing
their mind. It's a woman's prerogative, isn't it?

Most women develop a healthy sense of humor concerning
the cyclical nature of life. It is culturally acceptable, even expected that there are days when women are up — and days they
are down.

Men, however, are taught to believe that they should always
be in peak form. As The Code reinforces, winning performances
aren't everything, they're the only thing.

A number of men try to shake off the notion that there is
such a thing as male mid-life crisis. One male reader of my
column looked at mid-life as ridiculous — something that couldn't
be happening to him. In his words:

Dear Dr. Towery:

I am in my early forties, and I'm sick and tired of my wife and the women in the office talking about "male menopause." There's no such thing, medically or in any other way. Age can take its toll, but that certainly doesn't mean men go through a change like women do. All the same, women like to think it does happen. If I don't want to cut the grass, my wife teases me about not being able "to cut it" anymore. How can I shut them up about "male menopause"?

Often other people notice changes in our behavior before we do. Women are particularly astute at noticing changes. It isn't possible to "shut them up" as this man asks because we do change as we age. Dr. Edmond C. Hallberg coined the phrase, "the Male Metapause Syndrome" in his book *The Gray Itch*.[62] And he chronicles the changes in men as they reach middle age and beyond. Many of these changes are emotional. Men can become more obsessed with their performance orientation.

Part of this obsession with performance is a denial of old age. It appears to be a knee-jerk reaction because certain parts of their body no longer function as well as they used to. That is scary to many of us. Since men consider it a weakness to talk (and therefore admit that such things happen), they rarely get discussed.

The aging process

While men don't go through a dramatic hormonal change as women do when their production of estrogen stops, noticeable differences occur. A man at forty-five isn't the same as a young man at twenty-five. The fat content of the body increases. Vision changes make men more farsighted, causing many to don glasses for the first time.

The appetite begins to change as well. There are fewer taste buds, and more foods begin to taste bland. The cliché of a man always preferring his mother's cooking may simply be a case of his having better taste buds as a boy. Men begin to enjoy more pepper, more highly spiced food — if the stomach can take it.

A man's sexual style begins to change, too. Taking longer to achieve an erection, he usually takes longer to reach orgasm. Most women find this a pleasant switch, but men worry that it's the beginning of the end.

Age is the great equalizer; it catches up with everyone. It is inevitable that a period that marks the passing of some of his prowess is going to profoundly alter a man's way of thinking. He is living in a different world.

There had always been the hope that he could hit the "home run." He could always do better, to strive for the next achievement. As a result, men often become more obsessed with performance issues and run around trying to prove themselves. Such behavior might be called "middle-age crazy."

In speaking about women addicted to perfection, author Colette Dowling distills how it feels to be dominated by a performance orientation. She could well be talking about a man's mid-life crisis:

For the woman haunted by the fear of not getting enough recognition from others, performance becomes everything. Hers is the endless task of honing her skills, practicing, repeating past successes in an effort to keep the admiration coming. But any performance that is less than triumphant disturbs her inflated self-image, making her feel depressed and worthless.[63]

This is the uneasy feeling of men who are dominated by The Code experience. Real men, they reason, understand the importance of work. It defines the man. A successful man is one who does his work well. He wins. The voice inside tells him over and over again that he must *keep* winning.

Real men are calm, cool, and collected. No room here for a panic attack, let alone an extended bout of depression. True men don't complain or whine. If the muscles hurt from strain, that's nobody's business. "Playing hurt" is a source of pride to male athletes. Don't need anyone calling you a pussy. Men are supposed to *fix* it, not break down. "Get on with it," as the saying goes. "No matter how much it hurts."

The "real men" of The Code know that life is a game, and that they are not only supposed to be players, but *important* players. Women learn that it is okay to be on the sidelines at times; they learn to let go and admit that they aren't always at their best.

By comparison, you may hear one woman telling a friend over lunch that she had a terrible night. "I was looking my absolute worst," she might say. "And wouldn't you know it, I ran into my new boss at the movies." Or, she might confess that she felt really bad the other day and made the mistake of snapping her husband's head off for no real reason.

Men don't sit and make such confessions. If they do, they lace it with humor to throw you off the track. Inside they may be coming apart. You marvel at how "together" they are.

Real men tackle life at face value and learn early on to take care of business regardless of what it takes. And they do it, because real men have *balls*. Real men are always prepared to dig in, sweat and get the job done — or die trying.

The crisis of aging

It's no small wonder that mid-life crisis can cause major trauma. For the first time in his life, a man must look at his vulnerability to the aging process. Here's an enemy he can't punch, poke or kill. He is going to lose some of his physical agility, and that means he is apt to lose at one competition or another.

Until recently, we also assumed getting older meant losing some of our mental agility. Fortunately, the latest studies show quite the contrary. The brain is like a muscle and the more you exercise it with new ideas and problem solving the sharper you get.

When women tell men that society is much crueler to them as the aging process sets in, many men will puff out their chests and agree. "Yeah, we look distinguished with gray hair at the temples. Wrinkles add character and make a man's face ruggedly good-looking."

But underneath the pomp and pretense, is another man who is terrified of becoming useless. Terrified that he is going to be put out to pasture by the company. Terrified that he is no longer going to be attractive to anyone, even those who used to love him — his family. Who loves a loser?

While women often assume men are sitting in judgment of *their* aging process, lusting after firmer flesh and laughing at old ladies, the reverse is true. They're too busy recounting the indignities of the aging process for themselves. People talk about "helping little old ladies cross the street" in our society. Not men.

Men can't even cope with pain as well as women, although you would be hard pressed to find one to admit it. The thought of a chronic, painful illness is also more terrifying to men than women.

It's no wonder. The thought of becoming physically weaker or dependent on others for survival is excruciating to the male. Where's the chapter in The Code on "dependence on others"? There isn't one! After all, he's the guy who is supposed to get things done. He's the one who is supposed to take care of others.

The threat of impotence

Coupled with the notion of growing weaker is the obvious soft spot for the male: What if he can't get it up anymore? One newspaper editor claims the pressure to perform is compounded by male peers: "I think men are conditioned by other men to believe that the sum total of their masculinity is the ability to have an erection. When they don't, it's all over."

So he's read in some book that it will take longer between erections. But what if it never comes up? It doesn't take a rocket scientist to predict the man's response: "My God, it *is* all over. "That's it. I'm getting useless.

It's no wonder that the male will do anything — including rounding up some younger women — to prove he still has it in him. The male ego is made of fine china. The reason is simple. No one has ever trained him to accept defeat. More importantly, he has never trained himself to accept it.

Hopefully, as men break through the silence of The Code, they will realize that they aren't alone. They will see that men have a heavy load to face in mid-life, but it isn't all downhill.

Once a man comes to terms with his own mortality and his physical and emotional vulnerabilities, new possibilities open up. He *can* cut back at the office. He *can* spend more time with his family. He *can* take life a little more slowly and savor each moment along the way.

The fear of being alone

Positive change will occur slowly. Men aren't going to open up all at once. While the women's movement over the past twenty years has opened an unprecedented number of new opportunities for females, men have been slow to react. The American male is in transition, and it will take some time for him to catch up.

There is a tenacious myth that men can survive just fine after the loss of a partner. People are more inclined to worry over a widow than a widower. Children, it seems, even tend to think Dad can do okay. And they are shocked when they realize they have made a mistake.

Dear Dr. Towery:

I am writing for advice about my father. Mom died about a year ago and I don't think my Dad is doing well. He stays to himself most of the time. He retired four years ago and never did much except take trips with Mom. When I call he is nice, but far away, if you know what I mean. It's like he is falling into a tunnel and I can't reach him.

I am an only child and I sometimes think it would have been better for my Dad to have a son instead of a daughter. We've never communicated well. What do most retired men do when their wife dies?

The reader isn't alone in thinking men can hold up better when their spouse dies. In reality, men are simply better at hiding their feelings. Whether a man would become closer to a son than a daughter is impossible to say. Actually, the father-son relationship is one of the toughest of all relationships, while a father-daughter relationship isn't as complicated. Many girls report that they know their fathers better than anyone and feel closer to the father than sons do.

In general, one of the best ways to help a loved one move through the grieving process is to recognize that it is indeed a process and the grief won't go away overnight. Second, it's important to offer helpful suggestions of things to do and see. But don't try to bully them into going out just to go.

The father previously described is typical rather than unusual in his reaction. Most men do pull in when they feel sad. "Better to be alone than for others to see you sad or down," according to The Code. However, after making sure that a parent knows you are there for them and giving them a few suggestions on things to do, there is little else you can do. It may take months before he takes you up on a suggestion. What is important is showing that you care.

The male's Achilles heel

In one area men are more vulnerable. They are generally more afraid of being alone as they grow older. Statistics show that widowers typically die within a few years of their spouse, perhaps indicating that men are less able to cope with being alone — especially as they age. Also, women are taught to cope with a larger number of life's experiences and have intimate friends to help them do so. Men typically put all of their emotional eggs in just two baskets: work and family.

There are other reasons that the widower may have more trouble adjusting. The female partner usually represents the social fulcrum of his life. She makes up most of the rules as they go along. Defining the couple is ordinarily the woman's responsibility. She establishes the lifestyle, the routine that is the anchor of their life together.

It is understandably so. Even in primate societies, the females set the rules and they keep things going. The male's highest duty is to protect the females, for without them, the group would die.

In comparison, there is nothing in the background of most males to prepare them for the relationship experience. When a man makes the initial steps towards intimacy, he often becomes afraid that he is weakening. On one hand, is the traditional woman getting her sense of self-worth from being loved. On the other, is the man who has a fear of entering into a love relationship.

Although most men spend a great deal of time hiding their dependence on women, it is well-documented that they don't do well without them. In fact, many go off the deep end or die. Clinical studies show that the man who loses his female partner, whether through divorce or death, is more vulnerable to mental illness, suicide, or death than the woman in a similar situation.[64] A bachelor with no stable partner also faces a higher risk in these areas.

In comparing single men to single women, divorced men to divorced women, or widowed men to widowed women, the men are more likely to end up in a mental institution in each case. Statistics indicate that the divorced male has an annual death rate that is more than *three* times higher than the divorced female.

Why a man doesn't do well alone

When women speak of the fear of being alone as they age, they are not alone in their fear. Men have grave reason to be afraid.

Men tend to focus more exclusively on their female partners and their work. As they age, both are put in jeopardy. There's probably a young guy — or a young woman — at the office who understands his job better than he does. He is losing his edge and he knows it.

In his relationships he has probably failed in several areas: he probably isn't as close to the children as his wife; he probably has few (if any) close male friends; the majority of his social contacts are probably other couples that his wife picked out.

If he belongs to social clubs or has poker playing buddies, the ties are probably superficial. No wonder he is bereft when the woman goes.

In addition, he probably doesn't even know how the household operates. He isn't familiar with the little tasks that keep things moving smoothly. He has been taken care of, protected by a female partner who watched after the details. When the children are sick, it is not uncommon for the mother to take care of things — sometimes without even "worrying the father" about the details. As couples grow more equal in their partnerships, this is changing, but as most women will attest, the change *is* slow.

The same man who can change a tire, probably doesn't know what kind of soup his children like to eat. The same man who presents a multimillion dollar proposal to a bank's board of directors may have no clue where his wife buys his pima-cotton shirts. He may think his socks magically travel to the clothes hamper. And the list goes on. He may not even know when his mother's birthday is — his wife always takes care of that for him.

Breaking out of the useless syndrome

Without a doubt, the mid-life crisis represents a crucial phase for men. It is often triggered by men's first glimpse of their own mortality. But there is a promising note if they choose to see it: they can begin reassessing their lives in terms of emotional bonds rather than work.

Every gray hair need not become a testament that he is not as strong or as virile as a younger man. Looking positively at the second half of life, however, requires letting go of the old scorecards. It requires understanding that life is full of possibilities — as long as one believes it is.

Men who live the longest are often those who enter fields they love and continue to devote time and energy to those efforts, literally until the day they die.

But men are going to have to learn to be tough in a new way. Emotional rewards are generally commensurate with risk. And this is a tough challenge because the man's basic training is to hold it in, to *not* communicate.

Yet, being open is the best path to a full-bodied relationship, one that promises a full sharing of life's dramas. That's why men need to drop the scorecard mentality. It's ironic, but it's important to realize how much you lose by always focusing on winning.

CHAPTER TWENTY-FIVE

DOWN WITH THE HAWKEYE MYTH

*Question for women: Do you think of Alan Alda as the mascu-
line ideal — a funny, sensitive, perfect
man?*

Hawkeye to a young new nurse at the M*A*S*H camp:
"Want to play sardines tonight?"
"Sardines?" she asks demurely.
"My tent. I'll even bring the oil," he says.

The illusion that fools

Hawkeye Pierce has been identified as the prototype of the
new man. Women point to Hawkeye and say, "That's the way a
man should be: funny, self-effacing, sensitive. He can see through
the horrors of war. He doesn't enjoy picking up guns and fighting
like other macho nerds."

The list of Hawkeye's good qualities seems endless. He's
sexy, witty, liberated, open, charismatic, knows what he wants,
where he's going, and how he's going to get there. And on top
of all that, he's simply adorable. In short, this is the guy who can
help all the other male Neanderthals find their way. He's broken
through all the bull.

I wonder how many men have had the silver-tongued
M*A*S*H renegade thrown in their face while trying to slurp a
beer and doze through a football game in peace. And it's not just
women. When searching for an agent for my book, I was told by
one man that the macho male problem had been effectively eradi-

cated by the Hawkeye role — and that happened ten years ago. In other words, men and women are now on the same wave length, all thanks to Hawkeye's teachings.

Yet, something has never rung quite true to me about this character, but I couldn't quite figure it out. So I sat down to watch a few episodes of M*A*S*H to discover his great appeal to women, and this is what I saw:

- *Commitment phobic* — Hawkeye doesn't get involved. He has sex, smooches, talks sweet talk to women. But it's always on his terms, his timetable, leaving no doubt that he is not going to commit to anything — except to being a great physician. His work. Sound familiar?

- *Boozer* — Hawkeye doesn't waste his time on the traditional military anesthetic, beer. He heads straight for the hard stuff, in his tent where he distills it. Dry martinis. Straight up. No wimpy vermouth for the sensitive surgeon.

- *Sex Sporter* — So many nurses, so little time. The camera hones in on wiggly bottoms and breasts and then pans in on a Hawkeye whose expression can't be mistaken for anything but pure lust. The bloody veteran of the operating table is understandably exhausted after saving half of the regiment from what would have been sure death at the hands of a less capable surgeon. What does he need to make him whole again? A woman. Just any woman? Heavens no. A new woman. Not new as in liberated, but new as in one he never tried before. No matter that sex for sport is a defense mechanism against intimacy and commitment. He's sooo cute.

- *Winner* — Whatever else Hawkeye Pierce is, he is first and foremost a winner. Nobody gets the best of him and woe be to those who try. When Hawkeye is crossed, the rule book goes out the window. Suddenly, nothing is as important as coming out on top. His vengeance is such great fun. Whether it's ruining a career, breaking a heart, or just dumping on silly Frank and Hot Lips, our boy is the host with the most. Losing is not in his vocabulary.

- *Independent Cuss* — No stupid army regulations are going to interfere with our hero's lifestyle. He is an individual, part of no amorphous group like the army. This is a man who goes his own way. If you are going to have the pleasure of his company, that's just the way it's got to be. "I've just got to do this my own way," says Hawkeye. Sounds more like John Wayne than the new man. But how can you mention an anachronism like "The Duke" in the same breath as the new male role model?

- *A Man's Man* — In one episode, Radar says the equivalent of "Gee, Hawkeye, you've got to keep your head on straight, 'cause we all depend on you. You're our leader." A bigger shoulder. Someone who can always be counted on to carry the load. No matter what the emotional toll, a man who gets the job done. If we didn't know better, we might see Hawkeye as the typical corporate workaholic, shouldering everyone's burdens, waiting for a heart attack to happen. Naaah, he's too slick to fall into that trap.

But that's the problem. Because the only thing that separates Hawkeye from The Code is his slick talk. In the end, even that lets him down. In the final episode Hawkeye suffered what might be the equivalent of a young man's heart attack: he had a nervous breakdown.

What did we expect when his acceptance came from that ancient and deadly male formula — performance for lovability? One could reason that when Hawkeye realized he no longer had the M*A*S*H unit to take care of, his work (and therefore his worth) was finished.

What does a defunct TV show in its rerun period matter? Because the illusion is poisonous. Men are still compared unfavorably to a character who masqueraded as something new. Yet, he appealed to women in the most traditional of male ways. He was a performer, a winner. He could stand alone. He gave lip service to being sensitive, but he moved from one cute nurse to the next. They were there for his pleasure. They were either putting his gloves on for him, draping a surgical smock over his sensitive shoulders, feeding him sandwiches, or going to bed with him.

Talk about mixed messages. Tell men you want a sensitive teddy bear and then trot out a dagger-witted, high-achieving, always victorious Don Juan as your example, and watch their blood pressure go up — and their confidence go down.

Almost everything about Hawkeye is macho. Oh, he makes fun of the traditional male values. Yet he benefits from them more than anyone else on the show. The women always wait for Hawkeye. He's Number One. How many average guys have beautiful women constantly coming on to them? How many men can be surrounded by so many buddies — buddies you can put down endlessly but love you just the same. The whole enigma of Hawkeye, on closer scrutiny, is The Code. And it's The Code in bold face.

None of this is liberation. It needs to be acknowledged for what it is. Something is wrong here. The whole thing is convoluted. There's no equality — he gets any girl he wants. He is a total performer, and women love him for it. Verbally, he is self-effacing, which throws you off center. He *seems* like a good, kind-of-humble guy. In reality, he's just another traditional male, repackaged in an arty, pseudo-sensitive mask.

He's one more male renegade who sticks it to the establishment. He's always making fun of the people in charge. And he can do it because he's so good. If he wasn't a great surgeon, wasn't a quick wit, wasn't a great lover, he would lose his appeal.

What if Hawkeye lost?

The one time he did lose — that was the end. The show

closed with Hawkeye losing it all. He had a nervous breakdown. And there is another painful message for men: When you lose control, it's over.

Then women ask me why men won't open up? Why won't he say he's lost? Why won't he tell me when he's down. Because of shows like M*A*S*H. Because we, all of us men and women, really haven't broken through the illusion quite yet.

CHAPTER TWENTY-SIX

A PROMISE FOR THE FUTURE

Question for men and women: In the never-ending battle of the sexes, is it possible to bridge the differences?

Absolutely. Men and women can reach a greater understanding of their inherent differences, learn from each other, and learn to complement one another in partnerships.

But a breakthrough can only be achieved when the power of The Code is acknowledged, and then dispelled.

"A man in armor is his armor's slave."

As Robert Browning noted a century ago, a man in armor is not a free man. A man who models his behavior under the dictates of The Code one day discovers that being male is very limiting. In effect, there is nothing more debilitating than living by maxims that prescribe little or no emotional sharing and promote winning at all costs. How can one deal with shortcomings if the first rule is to hide them?

As a group, men still find themselves carrying around an armor of self-sufficiency, spending the better part of their lives developing an illusion of always having the answers. Inevitably, the charade becomes empty and painful. They become slaves to the very armor they once shouldered to protect themselves.

Several factors have cornered the male into hanging on to unhealthy patterns: the lack of man-to-man intimacy, the anger of the more radical feminists, changes in acceptable sexual norms, and a seemingly unrelenting emphasis on material achievement.

Breaking out

Awareness. The first step toward breaking out of The Code is awareness. An awareness of the profound differences in men and women; an awareness of how tenacious The Code's dictates are. There are ways to bridge the gap, but awareness must be present before any techniques can be effective.

In my column, I write about people's fears, struggles, hopes, and even their despair. Many have told me that my column has made a positive difference in their lives. But when people write to me about a problem, I cannot say, "Go out and do this and everything will be okay." I wish it were that simple. Yet, it is simply the process of sharing that is most helpful.

A woman in her thirties wrote in about an incident of sexual harassment that had occurred when she was twenty-three years old. After relating the incident to her father, she was devastated by what she interpreted as his lack of concern. He simply asked, "Did he physically hurt you?" "No," she responded." "Do you like the job?" "Yes," she answered. "Well, then, forget about it. That's the best thing to do," he suggested.

But she hurt inside and felt humiliated. Since her father had been dead for several years, she could not go back and resolve her disappointment. I explained that her father was undoubtedly interpreting the incident in male terms. Since she was twenty-three years old, he felt the need to allow her to take more responsibility and learn to work things out more independently. If she had been his son, he probably would have inflicted this lesson at an even earlier age.

He undoubtedly realized that he would not always be there to protect or defend her. In practical terms, if she was not hurt and she did enjoy her work, then the typical male response is "to shake it off."

Many men do have difficulty identifying with the female's feelings of vulnerability and pain in these situations. We saw a powerful demonstration of this during the Anita Hill hearings over the alleged incidents of sexual harassment by Supreme Court Justice Clarence Thomas. The all-white, male panel of senators who listened to the testimony was often berated for their lack of understanding and empathy.

At this time we need to realize that men and women have a lot to learn from each other. Our perspectives are often different, and we can inadvertently hurt each other if we don't understand just how different these perspectives are.

After my response was published, the woman wrote again:

I never looked at my father's response in terms of the difference between males and females. It makes more sense that he wouldn't have acted very upset, or at least didn't let on. I wanted him to feel exactly the way I did, and I now realize that it wasn't possible. He couldn't feel my humiliation.

My point in relaying this story is to illustrate the beneficial effects of awareness. There are fundamental differences in how men and women respond to the same event. Believe it. We cannot move forward until we accept that as a given, and take more responsibility as individuals for empathizing with the opposite sex.

Empathy. Empathizing with our loved ones is, quite possibly, the greatest gift we can offer. Ironically, people usually need to do it the most when they are the least prepared, i.e., when they are angry at their partner. However, both men and women are faced with so many new options today in lifestyle and behavior that we have to struggle against confusion. Given the rapid cultural changes we have experienced over the last few years, most of us are often unsure what is appropriate masculine or feminine behavior.

It is not a question of letting men get away with being less sensitive, or forcing women to take responsibility for the emotional closeness of the relationship. But the point is that by accepting the different styles of communication, accepting the different methods of interpretation, we can spare ourselves countless headaches and heartaches. To do this requires empathy, as the following letter illustrates:

Dear Dr. Towery:

I love Ross and we plan to be married in a few months. We've been together for four years now, so love really isn't a question. We are in love, we both agree. My problem? He almost never tells me. The more I ask him, the more he seems to withhold saying it. He says I know he loves me and I must admit I do, but I want to hear it more. Why won't he say the words?

Ross is telling this woman he loves her, but it's just done in Male Talk, the only language he knows (and probably the only language he'll ever feel comfortable using). As we have observed, men often express their love to women the same way they talk to other men — very secretly. A man's "I can always count on you," or "I'm always at ease when I'm around you," can be the equivalent of the most passionate "I love you" a woman can whisper. Even a joke, like "I should have my head examined for hanging around you," can code into "I'm crazy in love with you."

Men think the overall feeling of love should speak for itself. Moreover, men believe that women should accept their gestures, looks, jokes, and subtle, oblique mutterings as their statements of affection.

To insist he say words that are not part of his communication repertoire is often asking the impossible, so it is important to remember that the Male Talk vocabulary does not provide him with words to express passions and feelings. But, that doesn't mean he doesn't have these feelings — he does. When women try to learn the language of men, they often hear a man express "I love you" — and in more different ways than they ever imagined.

There is a simple method to gaining greater empathy. The next time you think your partner is being unreasonable, and you are ready to launch into an argument, go off by yourself and make a list of his or her attributes. List the considerate things that they have done in the past few months. (If you can't think of one thing, yes, you might be in trouble.)

Seriously, think of what is right about the other person and weigh that against the indiscretion or bad deed they have allegedly committed. Try to reason their side of the case for them. You may still have a legitimate gripe. But you also have a better perspective that can form the basis for a reasonable discussion versus a fight that nobody will win.

If you've been in a relationship for any length of time, you also start hearing things in your partner's statements that aren't there. I haven't met anyone who doesn't do this, although most of us aren't aware of how we flavor what is said.

For example, every time one man mentioned he was due for a big raise, his wife looked incredulous. She said, "Really? Is that true?" Without meaning to do it, the wife was cutting the man's self-confidence. He felt she didn't think he was worth an increase and walked away hurt and angry.

Finally, a friend witnessed a replay of the discussion, and he saw the husband huff out of the room. "What did I do?" she asked innocently. "You just blew him away," the other guy said. "You act like you can't possibly conceive of him getting a raise." She didn't realize the impact of her questions. She was so used to not getting pay increases herself that she was afraid her husband would be disappointed when his didn't come through. She truly wondered why he felt so sure he was up for a raise. It had nothing to do with her estimation of his abilities.

Make a list. Therapists who specialize in treating addictive personalities through twelve step programs like Alcoholics Anonymous, often utilize a simple but effective procedure. They recommend making a "gratitude list" whenever you get loaded down with self-doubt or self-pity. "It's the dead last thing you want to do when you're low, but by the third or fourth entry, you always feel better," reports one therapist. "In fact, most patients come in and say, 'I thought that was the silliest suggestion I'd ever heard — until I tried it'."

Reaching out. For the male, reaching out involves a great effort. It goes against all of his ideas about being a man. The majority of men really do try. They desperately want to earn the respect of their loved ones and the people they work with. Most of them were taught to do this by portraying a Gary Cooper-type of silent strength.

On the other hand, they hear that the "new woman" wants a "new man" like the Alan Alda type, so they try to work the strength-with-sensitivity model into their daily actions. The result is often as incongruous as Hawkeye Pierce breaking in a horse for the Marlboro man.

Finding a healthy balance is a lifelong process. It isn't achieved in one day and no one can maintain it every day. But when we are aware that we need to reach out more to others to obtain a greater balance in our lives, we must then decide to work at it consistently until it becomes in integral part of our lives.

Men, as a rule, need to reach out in three distinct areas: (1) in terms of sexual intimacy; (2) in terms of emotional intimacy with women; and (3) in terms of friendship with other men.

On a positive note, most men do feel more comfortable with the "new" sexually responsive woman. It's sort of like playing baseball — who wants to play with someone who hates the game?

It is discouraging, however, to read constantly that men now feel more responsible for pleasing their partner, and that instead of creating more intimacy, the responsibility is a new source of pressure. For example, in a 1987 issue of *Psychology Today,* Herbert J. Freudenberger, Ph.D., says "[men] often experience this responsibility as a loss of control, as a source of vulnerability rather than a possibility of greater intimacy. The man performs sexually, but what does he feel as he performs? Since he no longer can be intimate in the old in-control way, the price of greater intimacy seems too high."[65]

Hopefully, this is the exception. In my work, I see the opposite. Women who are more knowledgeable about sexuality and care more about it are more sensitive to the male's needs, and, in fact, help him around the performance pressure. The following letter is one I received from a woman who wanted to help her husband work through his performance anxiety in the bedroom:

Dear Dr. Towery:

Barry and I have been married for 12 years. It has been a good marriage and we would both do it again. I love Barry and don't want another man, have never been involved with another man. Periodically, something goes wrong that I don't understand. Any time that everything doesn't go exactly by script, he is devastated. If he doesn't perform as he thinks he should, he gets terribly upset and wants to try again later . . . and the next day . . . and the next. Things tend to get worse rather than better and I dread his coming home.

After a few weeks things gradually return to normal. But, eventually, it happens again and the cycle repeats itself. He doesn't believe me, but I honestly don't care whether he has an erection or not. I don't want or need perfect performance, but I do need affection and love, simply to be held. Somehow these needs of mine get lost in his concern about his performance. He becomes obsessed with the technicalities and I become miserable. Is this unusual? What can we do?

The woman's use of the term "script" is an excellent choice of words. Barry was taught from birth what it means "to be a man." He was taught that men must behave in certain ways — play out their lives in accordance to the rules of a historical script, passed down from father to son. He, like most men, has integrated performing sex with reaffirming his manhood.

Engaging in sex for Barry resembles making a presentation to the board. If they accept his ad campaign, he is the toast of the company. A rejection sends him to the mail room. He has learned to equate performance with lovability.

Fear of failure is the greatest cause of sexual problems among men. Once a man experiences what he considers failure, the fear increases to the point that it blocks his ability to give or receive sincere feelings of love and affection. A loving partner can help him to understand the vicious cycle controlling his emotions.

There are many ways of making love, and a sensitive woman can help a man break the cycle. It is far better if a woman knows enough about sexuality, and cares enough about it, to let a man know what gives her sexual pleasure. Such a woman is more likely to reinforce the notion that a couple's greatest happiness is simply being together with neither one feeling that he or she must *do* anything.

In these instances, it is also beneficial to remind your partner of the Ann Landers survey that revealed an overwhelming number of women would choose a sincere hug over sex. For many men, this knowledge is sufficient to move out of the performance for lovability trap. Look them in the eye, shake them, tell them you love them and don't give a damn about how they perform. Mean it. It's the most wonderful news a man can receive.

CHAPTER TWENTY-SEVEN

LIVING, LAUGHING, WORKING
AS ALLIES

Question for men and women: Do you sometimes think we have
lost a basic sense of trust between the sexes?

Many men still fall short when it comes to achieving genuine emotional intimacy with women, and they are the first to admit it. Most men scratch their head and wonder what the feminine definition of "intimacy" is. The Code certainly doesn't prepare real men for the mushy stuff. The language of intimacy remains as foreign to many of these men as Greek.

Women seem to think they know it. During one long plane ride, the woman seated next to me (after discovering that I was an advice columnist) decided to let me know that her husband didn't understand intimacy.

Innocently, I asked: "Well, what is it your husband does that is so offensive?" Her response: "Every night he comes home, parks in front of the TV set, drinks beer, and becomes a couch potato!" Trying another question, I asked: "Have you ever talked to him about how this makes you feel?" This time she was even more emphatic: "I can't stand to be in the same room with him."

Yet, this man probably feels he is making a statement by simply being with this woman. "Being there" is an all-important quality to men and they don't necessarily define that as offering their undivided attention to their partner.

However, all men can learn from this beer-drinking buddy. A man needs to set aside relationship time and make it part of his daily routine. Many men don't know how to relax with a partner and allow the energy in the relationship to grow healthy and strong on its own. They think they have to do something. A fancy dinner at a restaurant has its place, but so does a walk together around the neighborhood. But just as they react with other men, they usually don't think of having lunch with their wives just to talk or to catch up.

At this point, men need to take the time to look at intimacy, realizing that relationships usually come with a certain amount of love and happiness coupled with anxiety and disappointment. Intimacy is a knowable quantity. Simply put, it is trusting another human being to see inside. It is sharing thoughts and feelings, but it is not dumping. The best example of dumping I know is the husband who runs home to tell his wife he's sleeping with her best friend. Why? It has little to do with intimacy or trust. He just wants to shift the pain of his guilt to his wife.

Does that mean intimacy is only for sharing what is good? No. It means moments of letting our guard down to say:

"That hurt because . . .

"Why do you always compare me with John? I hate John. Are you trying to tell me something?"

"Do you realize what you've done to the girls? They think you hate them because you grounded them."

"Are you sure you want to take that new job? Is it what you really want?"

We can't go through life or experience any relationship without a certain amount of pain. However, we can work through our feelings of misery instead of allowing them to engulf us. Self-pity, remorse, and anger are all negative emotions that need to be recognized and then disposed of by working through them.

The woman who doesn't say she is upset by her husband's repeatedly being late for dinner isn't doing him a favor. She's building a mother lode of anger — and it will find some way to surface. When it does, it is almost sure to be damaging. The guy who is tired of a huge mortgage payment and wants out isn't doing his wife a favor keeping it inside either. He's building up resentments. Resentments that might sneak out in other areas of the relationship. "You want to go to dinner?" he asks. "Great. We'll all go to Papa Leone's." (He knows she hates Italian.)

One man at a seminar said he knew when his first marriage was over:

> *Judy was good to me. She helped me get through med school by working two jobs. I never said much but I loved her for being there. I used to fantasize about how good it would be for us when I finished school and started making money.*
>
> *I looked in the refrigerator one day and there was no root beer. Judy knew I loved root beer. A bell went off. Judy had started to pull away. Other little signs followed. She was always too tired to make love. She couldn't meet me at the library to go have dinner together. I didn't know she was wearing out, that she couldn't stand the hours anymore and me always having my nose in a book. If she'd only said something. Maybe we could have turned it around.*

We will all improve our chances for partnerships when we realize that the opposite sex often represents our strongest ally while we find our way in the world. As syndicated writer Harry Stein once wrote, "in the never ending battle of the sexes, sometimes both of you win."[66]

The male's undeniable bond

Contrary to popular mythology, men are more dependent on women. In an article for *Glamour* magazine, Stein aptly describes the male's dependence (albeit a silent one) on the fairer sex: "Quite simply, reluctant as we may be to share the information with those to whom we are ostensibly closest, most of us men are acutely aware of the depth of our emotional dependence on the women in our lives; aware that they are our anchor, our surest ally, often our only link to the world beyond ourselves."[67]

He points to a survey conducted a few years ago in which 77 percent of more than 2,300 married men said that, given the chance, they would marry the same woman again. Interestingly, a comparable study by a women's magazine demonstrated that only half of the married women responding would choose to marry the same man.

Different expectations

The differential is perhaps the result of our respective expectations. The expectations are changing, but we still have a long way to go. Historically, the female entered into marriage expecting the male to deliver a brighter and larger package. He was expected to deliver a whole new way of life, and the byproduct of this way of life would be blissful happiness.

As today's women develop other aspects of their lives more independently, the former expectation is changing — and for the better. The historical expectations explain, in part, the female's more pronounced disillusionment with the opposite sex.

There is another component of the relationships that needs work. The male has been very adroit and practiced at withholding affection and verbal expressions of love and needs. This isn't because he wants to make the woman miserable, but because his rigorous, early indoctrination to The Code taught him he must retain these emotions, maintain his strength, i.e., his masculinity. After all, it was all downhill for Sampson after Delilah cut his hair. But on a positive note, I see the beginnings of men good-naturedly laughing at themselves and each other over these silent enigmas generated by The Code.

Accepting differences

There are other expectations that will not change overnight, and these we must simply be willing to accept as differences. The male's sexual needs appear to be more pressing than the female's. In men, the need for affection and intimacy are often inextricably tied to sex. It's one of the few places he lets his guard down.

Ironically, when he marries to fulfill this need, he often finds inconsistencies in his spouse. What happens if he lets his household duties slide? The wife may start to act coldly to him. He can feel the temperature drop and the effect on him may be to withdraw instead of deal with it.

But rejection within a marriage is more than a woman's "I have a headache, dear." A man wants to feel needed. He wants to play together. If he feels she is having sex to acquiesce to his needs, he will generally withdraw. Masturbation can take care of that itch.

One of the differences we must deal with is that men are more romantic initially, but that women, as a rule, are superior at maintaining romance. Research during the past two decades has demonstrated that men are definitely more romantic, falling in love more readily than women, and more likely to fall into unrequited love, notes Carin Rubenstein, Ph.D.[68] Moreover, men are more likely to have crushes, and claim they recognize feelings of love sooner than their partners do.

Until recently, men could literally *afford* to be more romantic than women, since men accepted the financial responsibilities of the marriage partnership and wouldn't dream of looking at the woman as a meal ticket. There was a name for men who didn't pay their way — gigolos. Rubenstein goes on to suggest that women may become more romantic as their own careers allow them the luxury to stop looking at men only for money and status.

Perhaps a generation from now, that might be true. But today's studies indicate that men still must jump through several qualification hoops to pass women's marital test.

On the other side of the coin, women typically assume the role of care giver, better prepared to soothe and empathize with people when they are hurting. Plus, she is more adept at demanding and achieving intimacy.

In marriage, men view their actions as proof of their love, while women tend to also want verbal reassurance. This is a source of endless frustration in relationships and won't be resolved until both people put themselves in their partner's shoes.

In this regard, men seem to stay a step or two behind women. And men appear to get in more trouble when they try to anticipate a woman's needs. Debra, a legal secretary, recalls the time her father bought a house for the family and how it set off a virtual explosion from her mother:

You would have thought my Dad had hit a homer in the World Series he was so excited. He bought my Mom the first home in a new subdivision. He was so pleased with himself and proud of what he had done.

He had neglected one important consideration, though, and I will never forget the fight he and my Mom had. She wanted to live in a different section of town and she never forgave him for signing the papers without her.

The above example proves an important point: We get ourselves into the most trouble when we try to play psychic. While he meant well, Debra's father was obviously in trouble by failing to discuss the decision with her mother. Men are particularly bad about this, since expressing emotional needs is so tough for them.

In different ways, we all do this with the people we love. The first step is to pull back when you realize you have donned your psychic hat, and understand that the most important consideration is what the other party wants, not what you decide they need. It is equally dangerous to expect your partner to play psychic about your needs.

Women can be culprits as well. One physician I interviewed recalls the year he bought his wife a car for her birthday in early

February. On Valentine's Day, he gave her flowers and a box of candy. At the time, she was overweight, and in his words, "She wouldn't talk to me for two weeks because she said I had been cruel to give her chocolates when she was on a diet. Of course, I didn't help myself any when I pointed out that she didn't have to eat the whole damn box at one sitting."

Assuming that your partner can read your mind, or that he or she can automatically be sensitive to your needs, is one of the surest ways to get into hot water. If you want intimacy, you need to ask for it.

The woman's edge

When it comes to knowing how to be a good friend, men can learn a lot from women. Many women spend hours each week nurturing their friendships. They call just to gossip, to say they're disappointed in the kids' grades, or complain that they have a headache and don't feel like working.

It is these little pieces of information that help our friends know who we are. It isn't our salary. It isn't our address or the car we drive. And it certainly isn't our golf handicap. We are the sum of our emotions, and we aren't really friends until we share them.

Finding our way to trust

While the differences at times seem insurmountable, there is assuredly light at the end of the tunnel. The modern male is faced with a growing ambiguity of roles, whether it is in his sexual relationships with women, his commitment to marriage and family, or his chosen line of work.

But the ambiguities are far outweighed by what men stand to gain when they refuse to be frozen by the tenets of The Code. It is an attitude that promises a man that he can be as close to his daughter as to his son; that says his daughter is as likely as his son to follow in his shoes or take over the family business; that says his wife is more likely to be an equal ally versus a dependent partner. She can hold up a mirror that reflects not how much he is diminished by this new equality, but how much he has gained. In the work place, he is more likely to encounter a new management style by women, a style more balanced in terms of human factors. Women managers don't sidestep people issues — they dive right in and deliver strong results in the process.

However, as society began to question the traditional male and female roles, it also lost something valuable in the process. We lost the feelings of trust between the sexes that went with those traditional patterns of behavior. When we lived in Ozzie- and Harriet-type roles, Harriet was trying to do her best to be a good homemaker, and Ozzie was doing his damnedest to be a good provider.

Trust is difficult to build when the media, and even society at large, are hitting us with hefty double messages. It is discouraging, for example, when Betty Friedan, author of the landmark feminist book, *The Feminine Mystique,* warns against what she calls "sequentialism," or leaving a career and resuming it after child-rearing.[69] Wasn't the point of the women's movement to increase the number of options?

Beyond pigeonholing

The time has come to build the requisite level of trust, and both sexes need to move beyond pigeonholing each other. No one has developed the final word on child rearing or daycare. And it doesn't advance our society to suggest that staying at home with the kids is a cop-out from dealing with child care and leave.

In fact, it should be an option that both men and women feel free to evaluate as a lifestyle, instead of fearing new labels or new economic consequences. To form absolute judgments about which behavior is acceptable and which is not is a return to the past, not a prescription for the future.

No more trenches

To move beyond our respective foxholes, we must let go of purely self-fulfilling goals and performance scorecards. It means *learning* and *teaching* the benefits of sharing, giving, and trusting. And this calls for a new brand of courage from both men and women. Katherine and Jack, a couple attending one of my seminars, demonstrate how this can be done.

Jack is a financial planner in his late thirties who grew up "in a very cold, unaffectionate family in Minnesota." Katherine, also in her late thirties and a production consultant, grew up in a close-knit Southern family in Alabama.

"For the first two years of our marriage, I think I cried every night," Katherine recalls. "When Jack was working at his desk at night, and I would try to go up and hug him, he would freeze up and act like I was doing something wrong. It really hurt. I had no idea my marriage would be like that."

But Katherine persisted. She believed in Jack's commitment to her and the marriage; and she had spent enough time with his family to realize why Jack was so uncomfortable with affection.

Her perseverance paid off. Gradually, Jack quit freezing up every time she showed him affection. And one day, he opened up and hugged her back.

Jack and Katherine have been married for fourteen years, and there have been ups and downs. But they are an affectionate couple who learned that they can work through things. As Katherine notes, "There is nothing like working through one problem to give you the energy you need to work through the next one."

Fear of Failure

Taking responsibility for our choices also means not being afraid of making mistakes. The following cliché is still valid: It isn't how many times you fall. It's how many times you get up that counts.

Today, young adults are waiting longer to marry, and when they do, they realize that more than 50 percent of the marriages will not last. Later in life the numbers get worse: six out of every ten second marriages end in divorce.

No wonder young people are dating more, committing less, and are more fearful than ever that a relationship might not work. In fact, the fear of failure coupled with the ease of extrication when the road gets bumpy can become a self- fulfilling prophecy. It also means a lot more hearts are broken. Jeanine, a thirty-four-year-old pharmaceutical representative relates the following:

When I was in college, my first love broke my heart. I went into the hospital for surgery, and he didn't even bother to come by to see if I had survived. I was devastated. I told my parents I wanted to quit school.

My mother asked me why I didn't want to go back to campus. And I told her I was too ashamed to face everyone, since everyone in school knew I loved Rob. My mother said: "Never be ashamed of loving someone. You can come to me and be ashamed when you can't love. That's when I will start to worry."

As Jeanine later told me, she has long since forgotten why she found Rob so intriguing. But she has never forgotten her mother's wisdom. We all feel humiliated when someone walks away from us, but our very vulnerability opens us up to all the possibilities of love.

Making a move

In making choices, sometimes we have to decide that it's time to move ahead. At this stage, whether it is a man or woman, it is often important to find sound, third-party advice. This can range from therapists to marriage counselors to ministers or to self-help books. It's more dangerous, though, to assume a problem will get better on its own. It rarely does. It's often tempting to believe that everything will be okay as soon as the *other* person changes. This is an easy trap to get caught in. And such an expectation is not only a myth, it's unfair to yourself and to your partner.

It takes two people to set up a negative pattern, and it takes two to move out of it. It is self-defeating to focus completely on the other person's shortcomings. If you find yourself saying, "If only she would change," or "If only he would be better," then you need to look inside of yourself. Once you've taken that step, then it is fair and reasonable to talk to the other person about what is upsetting you.

Providing miracles

One of the most liberating lessons we can learn is that no one person (or sex) has all the answers. You don't have to provide miracles for other people. Trying to be perfect all the time isn't going to make another person happy. And it's going to make you miserable. But neither should you expect other people to provide miracles for you. This improved attitude requires both sexes to recognize the tremendous social changes we are moving through and how difficult they are to assimilate.

To help each other out it's important to exercise patience, be forgiving, and give each other time to catch up.

Whether we realize it or not, all of us lapse into stereotypical thinking. It is better to develop our own internal checklist, and when we find ourselves thinking in older, inappropriate modes, we should try to do better the next time. One of the best examples of this is the woman who sighs and says, "I may as well not tell him. He would never understand my feelings. He would think I was being petty and jealous."

That's not fair. And it isn't going to make things better. Trying at least gives the couple a chance. Who knows? He may not only understand, but be delighted that she cares enough to be a little jealous.

We will all progress more quickly when we break our own negative patterns rather than point out those in others. It's far more productive than citing stereotypical behavior in others — a much easier task.

On balance, I think both sexes would agree that the changes are for the better — even if we admit so grudgingly. Today's men want a partner, not a prize isolated from reality.

Our lifestyles are very different from just five years ago, and they may change dramatically again in the next five years. In the midst of all these changes, we can't afford to lose sight of how we can be each other's best friend.

The sexists jokes aren't funny anymore. Men and women want to care, and they both do. Sometimes we can lose our way, though, and need someone else to help us get back on 'track.

While it's appropriate for each partner to have separate goals, it's also imperative to develop common dreams. A woman can strive for excellence in her job or profession. A man can dream of being the great American author, or the best tax accountant in a city. However, each must work at paving the groundwork for their mutual destination. And it doesn't matter if that mutual goal is investing in a racehorse or building a cabin in the woods. What matters is that the two people don't find reasons or excuses to grow in separate directions.

For better or worse, we live in a society that encourages self-development and self-fulfillment. Healthy development of self is important since it allows both partners to continue to bring something new to the relationship. However, a strong commitment to nurture mutual goals is the only way to keep the fabric of the relationship from unraveling.

Is it worth it? Never doubt it. And it is the better way to achieving greater understanding, intimacy, and trust, between a man and a woman.

NOTES

1. *Statistical Abstract of the United States,* 1990, pp. 80, 81, 83-85.
2. *Ibid.,* p. 83.
3. *Ibid.,* p. 80.
4. *Ibid.,* p. 75.
5. *Ibid.,* p. 75.
6. *Ibid.,* p. 81.
7. Carole Tavris, *Anger: The Misunderstood Emotion* (New York: Simon & Schuster, Inc., 1982), p. 119.
8. *Ibid.,* p. 119.
9. *Ibid.,* p. 127.
10. Michael S. Teitelbaum, *Sex Differences* (Garden City, NY: Anchor Books, 1976), p. 75.
11. Herb Goldberg, Ph.D., *The Hazards of Being Male: Surviving the Myth of Masculine Privilege* (New York: New American Library, 1976), p. 7.
12. Elizabeth Stone, "Sons and Mothers," *Savvy,* September 1988, pp. 114, 116.
13. *Ibid.*
14. *Ibid.*
15. *Ibid.*
16. Deidre S. Laiken, "When Couples Compete: Can You Be Lovers and Rivals," *New Woman,* March 1986, pp. 36-41.
17. Harriet B. Braiker, Ph.D., "Who Is the Right Man for a Woman Like You?" *Working Woman,* January 1987, pp. 72-74, 116-119.
18. Susan Jacoby, "When You're Smarter than He Is," *Cosmopolitan,* July 1988, pp. 144-147.

19. Gustave Flaubert, *Madame Bovary* (New York: Bantam Books, 1857), p. 168.
20. Braiker, *op. cit.,* pp. 72-74.
21. Mary Murphy, "I Have a Fear of Being Eclipsed," *TV Guide*, June 11-17 1988, pp. 27-32.
22. *Ibid.*
23. Evan Thomas with Pat Wiongert in Washington; Patricia King in Chicago; Nanny Abbott in Houston and Jeanne Gordon in Los Angeles, "The Reluctant Father," *Newsweek*, December 19, 1988, pp. 64-66.
24. *Ibid.*
25. *Ibid.*
26. Harriet B. Braiker, Ph.D., "Does Superwoman Have It the Worst?" *Working Woman,* August 1988, p. 65.
27. Philip Blumstein and Pepper Schwartz, *American Couples: Money, Work and Sex* (New York: William Morrow, 1983), p. 161.
28. Statistics cited by Arbitron Ratings Company, New York, New York, December, 1988.
29. Warren Farrell, Ph.D., *Why Men Are the Way They Are* (New York: McGraw-Hill Book Company, 1986), p. 96.
30. Wendy Reid Crisp, "Editor's Note," *Savvy*, October 1985, p. 4.
31. Carol Gilligan, *In a Different Voice, Psychological Theory and Women's Development* (Cambridge: Harvard University Press, 1982), pp. 41-42.
32. *Ibid.*, p. 14.
33. *Ibid.*, p. 15.
34. Hendrik Hertzberg, "The Short Happy Life of the American Yuppie," *Esquire*, February 1988, pp. 100-109.
35. Steven Naifeh and Gregory White Smith, *Why Can't Men Open Up?* (New York: Warner Books, 1984), p. 19.
36. Georgia Witkin-Lanoil, Ph.D., *The Male Stress Syndrome* (New York: Newmarket Press, 1986), p. 90.
37. Sara Bonnett Stein, *Girls and Boys* (New York: Charles Scribner's Sons, 1983), p. 20.

38. Marcia Cohen, *The Sisterhood* (New York: Simon and Schuster, 1988), p. 24.
39. *Ibid.*, p. 275.
40. *Ibid.*, p. 371.
41. Naifeh and Smith, *op. cit.,* "Acknowledgments," p. x-xi.
42. Jan Halper, "Monogamy Is Not a Natural State," *Cosmopolitan*, May 1988, pp. 164-166.
43. *Ibid.*
44. William Fezler, Ph.D., and Eleanor S. Field, Ph.D., *The Good Girl Syndrome* (New York: Berkley Books, 1985), p. 246.
45. Farrell, *op. cit.*, p. 311.
46. Donald H. Bell, *Being a Man, the Paradox of Masculinity* (San Diego: Harcourt Brace Jovanovich, Publishers, 1984), p. 34.
47. Edwin Arlington Robinson, "Richard Cory," *The American Tradition in Literature* (New York: Grosset & Dunlap, Inc., 3rd Edition), p. 1353.
48. Cohen, *op. cit.*, p. 370.
49. Carole Tavris, "Nine Myths about Men and One Truth," *Cosmopolitan*, March 1986, pp. 229-231.
50. Michael E. McGill, Ph.D., *The McGill Report on Male Intimacy* (New York: Harper & Row, Publishers, 1985), pp. 78, 108.
51. *Ibid.*, p. 14.
52. *Ibid.*, p. 9.
53. Maggie Haselwerdt, *Rock & Roll Confidential,* Newsletter, December 1988 issue.
54. *American Demographics,* December 1987, p. 16.
55. Privileged Information, July 15, 1989, p. 7.
56. Susan Jacoby, "35-plus and Aching for Sex," *Cosmopolitan*, March 1986, pp. 266-269, 275.
57. *Ibid.*
58. "How to Look Younger Longer and Stop the Clock," *Cosmopolitan* cover line, January 1989.

59. "Take Five Years (at Least) off Your Face," and "Our Hip & Thigh Diet (Exercises, Too)," *New Woman* cover lines, May 1989.

60. Barbara Foley Wilson and Charlotte Schoenborn, *American Demographics,* November 1989, pp. 40-43.

61. Colette Dowling, *Perfect Women* (New York: Summit Books, 1988), p. 240.

62. Dr. Edmond C. Hallberg, *The Gray Itch* (New York: Warner Books, 1977), p. 2.

63. Dowling, *op. cit.* p. 239.

64. Goldberg, *op. cit.,* p. 13.

65. Herbert J. Freudenberger, Ph.D., "Today's Troubled Men," *Psychology Today,* September 1987, p. 67.

66. Harry Stein, "Mates for Life," *Glamour*, April 1988, pp. 106-109.

67. *Ibid.*

68. Carin Rubenstein, Ph.D., "How Men and Women Love," *Glamour*, April 1986, pp. 282-283; 356-361.

69. Signe Hammer, "25 Years that Shook the World," *Ms.,* December 1988, pp. 51-58.